I0006714

BLOG IDEAS

131 IDEAS TO KILL WRITER'S BLOCK,
SUPERCHARGE YOUR BLOG AND STAND OUT

STEVE ALVEST

Copyright © 2016 StormShock Press (press.stormshock.com). All rights reserved.

Proofreading by Afterwords Communications (www.afterwordscommunications.com)

Cover design by Owais Zaman (99designs.com/profiles/2937996).

"Workspace in Cartoon Style" cover graphic created by Freepik (www.freepik.com)

Please do not copy any part of this book without written permission from the author. You may quote brief passages with attribution.

The information in this book was accurate at the time of publication. While the author has attempted to verify all information, neither the author nor the publisher assumes any responsibility for errors, omissions, or contrary interpretations of the subject matter herein.

CONTENTS

Join StormShock   v

1. Introduction   1
2. Ideas for Blog Topics   11
3. Ideas for Setting Up Your Blog   41
4. Ideas for Running Your Blog   57
5. Ideas for Blog Posts   77
6. Ideas for Getting Traffic   93
7. Ideas for Monetizing   113
8. Ideas for Coming Up with Ideas   129
9. Conclusion   145

Have You Joined the Mailing List Yet?   147
More on Blogging   149
About the Author   157
Also by Steve Alvest   159

JOIN STORMSHOCK

Want to see secret blog posts, get free and discounted books, and receive updated content about blogging and other topics? Join the Storm-Shock e-mail list.

It's free. I'll keep your email secret. Unsubscribe at any time.

And you'll also get access to some downloadable goodies.

Subscribe at www.smshock.com/list

Chapter 1

INTRODUCTION

I had a blog in 1997. It wasn't WordPress because this was years before that was even an idea. It was on a platform called GeoCities. GeoCities was a free website hosting service. Back then, people didn't have blogs. They had personal homepages.

My homepage had clippings of things I found interesting. Some snippets of JavaScript code. A few lines of markup teaching basic HTML. Funny pictures of my dog that I scanned from 4x6 photographs on my scanner. It was blogging before blogging became a thing.

I was a freshman in college with an undeclared major. I didn't know what to do with my life yet. My high school teachers thought I should go into art because drawing and creativity seemed to be my best talents. My parents would never have supported that, so I had to decide between computer science and chemical engineering. Both those majors would have appeased my parents, though they hoped I'd choose an engineering major. They preferred that I didn't become a computer nerd, but that's what I was. I opted to study computers because I had such varied interests. You can combine any field with computers. Art on computers. History on computers. Sports on computers. I can't say the same about chemical engineering. How do you do art with chemical engineering?

It was this spirit of combining two unrelated fields to make something new that sparked my creativity. No idea is original. They all build upon a base of past ideas just as you would build a pyramid out of blocks. A new idea cannot exist without the foundation of many old ideas beneath it. I looked to computers to build the base of my idea pyramid.

I discovered that computers would let me take part in any field. I could use my knowledge of computing to practice art. Or learn about ancient history. Or write. I could build anything I wanted upon this base. It was the foundation upon which I could test any idea.

Soon after everyone started getting on the internet, I

discovered blogging. It wasn't called blogging at the time, but I found that I could express any idea to the world by updating a personal homepage every day. I could write anything and share it with a world of strangers. And the things I wrote on my homepage might help some of those strangers. That was a good feeling.

Over the years, GeoCities and personal homepages went out of fashion. I had started experimenting with some of the newer content management software. My blog went through drastic changes between platforms like PostNuke, Gallery, and b2/cafelog. I even created a custom blogging platform while in graduate school. It ran my blog for a couple of years until I discovered WordPress.

WordPress made me abandon development of my custom blogging platform. It had it all, and I couldn't compete. It's like WordPress gave me a blank canvas on which I could create anything I wanted. All I had to do was imagine what my website would be, then make it happen on Word-Press. I would choose colors and how to lay things out. Then I would apply the brush strokes. These were the settings, themes, and plugins. I would paint until my vision became a reality. If the look that I envisioned for my site didn't exist, I could just create a new theme from scratch. If I had a great idea that nobody else had, I could write a plugin to make it happen in WordPress.

With blogging, we've combined ideas of computing with ideas of writing. We've laid a foundation of computing down with a layer of writing on top of it to make the solid base we call blogging. This book will show you some of the idea blocks you can use to build your blog.

~

Misadventures in blogging

My early attempts at blogging were like throwing darts in the dark. I would post anything that was interesting or amusing. My blogs had no direction. There was no target. I would do a complete revamp of my website every few months. New software, new style, and new content.

None of those blogs had any readers besides a few close friends. In hindsight, I realize my early blogs failed because they didn't have any focus. There was no reason for someone to visit my blogs. They were personal homepages filled with random thoughts and rants.

As with many amateur bloggers, I blogged whenever I felt like it. Sometimes I would post an article every day. Other times I would stop posting for months.

I once had a baseball card blog that gained a small following of daily readers. It wasn't a lot of traffic, but it was enough to pay the hosting bills with Google AdSense advertising. I scheduled a post every day for about two years. Then, when things got more hectic at my day job, I stopped posting for a couple of months.

When things got less busy at work, I came back to my blog. It was a ghost town. The readership disappeared. Internet silence greeted my new posts. I was writing to no one.

I made many mistakes like these over my years of blogging. Most of the time, I was just grateful that I stayed at my day job. Blogging is a constant struggle for traffic. Traffic comes from great content. Great content comes from ideas.

What's in this book

This book won't tell you what a blog is. It won't give you instructions for installing WordPress. It will not lecture you on how to create a proper blog. The purpose of this book is to give you ideas.

I'm sure you already have a blog or are thinking of making one. Whether you're a beginner or veteran blogger doesn't matter. There are ideas here that anyone can try. Some of the ideas are current best practices. Other ideas sound interesting in theory. And others are just plain crazy. You should have fun blogging. Otherwise, it's too easy to quit.

WordPress is the standard for blog platforms. About 60% of websites that use a content management platform use WordPress. While this book assumes most readers use WordPress for their blogs, you will still find this book helpful if you use something else. You can apply most of the ideas to any platform, whether it's Typepad, Tumblr, or even Facebook.

Everyone has creativity. It doesn't matter if you have a down-to-earth, logical mind. Anyone with a brain can be creative. This book has dozens of ideas to get you thinking. And once you get thinking, the creativity will flow.

Many blogs fail because the blogger stopped coming up with new ideas. This book will give you ideas and solve your writer's block once and for all. In this book, you will get ideas for blog topics. You will get ideas for how to set up and run your blog. You will find ideas and prompts for blog posts. There are chapters for getting traffic, engaging readers, and making money. And the last chapter will teach you how to find even more ideas.

Read through the ideas. Then, in the words of Bruce Lee, "absorb what is useful, discard what is not, add what is uniquely your own." I hope this book will at least add some color to the gray matter in your head.

How to use this book

This book is a reference guide. Open it whenever you find your blog spinning its wheels in the sand. Flip through its pages whenever you come down with a bad case of writer's block. Go to the chapter with the ideas you need and look through a few of them. That will be enough to jog your brain.

You can read this book cover to cover. You can also flip to the relevant section and cherry-pick which ideas you like. You can use it like a book, or a catalog, or a reference guide. The chapters are in the order you will need them.

Check out the *Ideas for Blog Topics* section before you start a blog. It will give you ideas for blogs and websites you can create. It is projects you might want to start for yourself. It will take you through ideas for several types of blogs you can start. Then, once you have an idea, it will give you ideas for finding hosting and getting a great domain name.

After you have a topic and domain name, *Ideas for Setting Up Your Blog* will give you ideas for setting things up. It will provide lists of useful plugins to consider installing. It will suggest functions you might want to include in your blog. And it will give you some tips on how to design your blog so visitors will like what they see.

Ideas for Running Your Blog will give some pointers on how you can build useful blogger habits. You will learn how to develop a productive writing discipline. Then it will show you some tools bloggers use to work better. Finally, it will give some tips for running a professional blogging business.

Once you're ready to start writing blog posts, you will need to come up with topics to write about. *Ideas for Blog Posts* will show you different types of blog posts you can write. It will give you ideas for what you can write about, no matter what niche you're in. You will find dozens of prompts to kickstart your creativity.

After you've written about 10-20 posts, you should pay some attention to finding readers. It isn't motivating to keep writing to a nonexistent audience. *Ideas for Getting Traffic* will help you bring readers to your blog. It will also cover some tips to optimize your blog for search engines. Then it will go over how you can use social media to engage readers and drive some traffic to your blog.

If your blog gets enough traffic, you can make money from your hard work. *Ideas for Monetizing* will show you some techniques that professional blog-gers use to make money. It will provide an overview of advertising and sponsorship sources. It will also go into affiliate marketing. And it will give some ideas for selling products and services through your blog.

This book has a limited number of ideas. But if you master your thinking skills, your well of ideas will never run dry. *Ideas for Coming Up with Ideas* can help you sharpen your thinking to come up with ideas on a consistent basis. It will also give some ideas for sources of inspiration. Then it will teach you some useful brainstorming techniques.

Chapter 2

IDEAS FOR BLOG TOPICS

A hook is the broad idea of your blog. It is like an elevator pitch. It is what you tell someone when they ask, "So, what's your blog about?"

One blog I built finally gained a fair number of readers. It was because it had an interesting hook: baseball card collecting. The hook was, "I have hundreds of unopened baseball card packs from the past 25 years. I'll open one pack a day." The audience was tiny, but for the first time, I had regular readers. Finding your blog's hook might be the most important decision you make.

Other important decisions include where you host your blog and the web address you choose for it. The host you choose affects your site's reliability, speed, and features. The web address is often readers' first impression of your site.

This chapter will provide ideas for choosing a hook for your blog. Then it will show you some hosting options to consider. Finally, it will give you some techniques for finding a proper web address.

Finding your hook

There are an infinite number of ideas out there. You must pick one and run with it. This section will help you pick an idea for your blog's hook.

For your blog to be successful, it should stand out somehow from the 300 million blogs that are already online. Don't copy or regurgitate. Give to the internet something that is unique to you. The only way to gain readers is to offer something that is not available anywhere else on the internet. Writing a blog is only worth your time if you have readers.

Before you do anything, you need a reason to do it. It's not enough to start a blog to make money. Making money is not a reason—it is a result. It's like saying, "I want to be a famous author." But that ignores the fact that you must be an unknown writer before you can be a famous one. So, cross "making money" off your list of reasons for starting a blog. You need to think deeper.

Think about your blog's topic. What kinds of people do you want to read your blog? What do you want to tell the world? What makes you want to wake up in the morning? It goes against intuition, but the narrower your idea is, the easier it will be to gain an audience. The journalist Herbert Bayard Swope once said, "I can't give you a sure-fire formula for success, but I can give you a formula for failure: try to please everybody all the time." If you fall into the trap of writing for everyone, no one will read your blog.

A niche is a specialized area of a broader topic. It is a subtopic that not everyone is interested in, but the audience can still be quite large. An example of a niche is "men who wear ties." Not many women, children, or casually dressed men will visit your blog. You might think you wouldn't get much traffic after alienating so many people, but the millions of people who still fit into the niche will be much more enthusiastic about finding the blog. And millions of people is not a tiny audience.

People find blogs by searching for specific keywords. If someone wants general information, they will go to one of the well-known big sites. It is when someone is looking for specific, niche information that they go to a search engine. Once on a search engine, they might find your blog even though they've never heard of it. Narrow down your blog topic as much as possible, and find your niche. A great hook always rests within a compelling niche.

You're good at something. Perhaps you have the sweetest basketball layup anyone in your neighborhood has ever seen. Maybe you follow political news and have controversial views for the next election. Or perhaps you have a knack for finding the best deals in town. Everybody is awesome at something, but not everybody knows it.

Your job is to find out what you're awesome at and write about it. You're awesome at that one thing because you're passionate about it. You're so passionate about it that you're willing to spend time on it to become excellent at it. If you're having trouble finding your passion, just ask someone close to you what you do best. Another approach is to think about what you can talk about for hours. If you can talk about something, then you can write about it, too.

There are many different types of blogs. Once you choose a topic for your blog, you need to craft the hook. Later in this chapter, you will find some ideas for how you can twist your topic idea into a hook.

Idea #1: Teach your skills

You know a lot more than other people do about at least a few subjects. You have hobbies or jobs that most people don't have. Share the information you know on your blog. People enjoy learning new skills.

For example, you can teach people how to live a self-sustaining lifestyle. If you know a lot about managing money, you can show people how to handle their personal finances. If your expertise is string theory, write a blog that simplifies it so even a beginner can learn.

Pick a topic you know a lot about. Think about some techniques you've discovered that might not be common knowledge. Give step-by-step instructions. This idea also lends itself well to creating online courses and YouTube videos.

Idea #2: Write about your journey

Set a big goal, and write about your journey towards achieving it. Turn your blog into a journal, and let people follow along on your mission. For example, do you take part in races like the Spartan Race and Tough Mudder? Start a blog about your goals and how you train for those races.

Idea #3: Teach the tools of your trade

What tools do you use most? They might be specific software like Evernote, physical tools like duct tape, or product lines like the Apple Watch. Write tips for using your favorite tools. Guide people, step by step, through performing certain tasks with the tools. Your blog can become daily reading for other individuals who have to use the tools every day.

Whatever your field, you can experiment with different techniques and software. Blog about what you discover. If you work in an office, what methods and software make you more productive? What didn't work out for you?

Idea #4: Run an experiment

What are some unique experiments you can try for your blog? You might be in a unique situation where you can try something out. We're not talking about lab experiments here. It doesn't even have to be anything risky or dangerous. Switching to a vegan diet? Write a blog about your struggles. On a quest to eat at every restaurant in your town? Blog about that. Buying a new television? Write a blog about how you choose. Test different things. Tell your readers what works and what doesn't.

Idea #5: Target a specific demographic

Jezebel is a popular blog for women. Kotaku is a blog for video game players. Target a particular demographic of people. To further narrow your focus, you should combine your chosen demographic with any topic. The advantage of this type of blog hook is that you know exactly who your intended audience is.

There are many kinds of demographics. You can target a physical trait like ethnic background, gender, or left-handedness. You can write for a particular occupation. There are also niche groups you can target like horse owners, cosplayers, or beach bums.

Idea #6: Write a book as a blog

A lot of books start out as blogs. The author of a popular blog might take several popular posts and compile them into a book to sell. What if you flipped that idea on its head? You could write a book and release it as a blog. Instead of publishing a fantasy novel as a book, you could release a chapter every week as a blog post. You can then polish the finished blog post book and publish it as a book. Your blog can be an ongoing story.

A twist on this idea is to think of your blog as a television drama. Post a new chapter or episode every week. End each season with a season finale to complete a book. Make sure every episode ends with a cliffhanger to keep readers waiting for the next blog post.

Idea #7: Write a reference guide book

Compile a reference guide as your blog. You can collect recipes to add to your cookbook blog over time. Maybe every month you can introduce a new chapter. One month you can write poultry recipes and the next month you can write soup recipes. This idea works for other types of reference material as well. You could compile a reference guide to the various types of zombies. Or all the different games produced by Nintendo. Every year or so, you can compile your posts into an e-book.

Finding a blog host

Once you have a hook for your blog, you need a host. The host is where your blog will live. It is a server computer at a data center somewhere in the world. Whenever someone loads your blog, their computer downloads it from the blog host.

There are many kinds of blog hosts. The easiest ones to set up are the free blog platforms like Tumblr or Blogger. Traditional hosts like GoDaddy or Host-Gator offer the most control but can be hard to set up. Managed WordPress hosting provides a good middle ground. They combine the ease of free blog platforms with some of the control of traditional hosts.

If you are blogging as a hobby, a free blog platform would be enough for you. No need to spend any of your hard-earned cash. All you have to do is choose a free blog platform, sign up, follow the directions, and be on your way. The biggest disadvantage of using a free blog platform is that you won't have your own domain name. Many of them don't let you add advertisements or use your blog for commercial purposes. Furthermore, free blog platforms don't give you much control. They reserve the right to change or delete your account whenever they like. There is nothing you can do about it. If that scares you, you should consider a paid blog host.

If you are willing to spend some money, traditional hosts start at just a few dollars a month. You buy one of their hosting plans, and they will set up some space for you on one of their server computers. This option offers the most control. It is perfect for bloggers who want to add custom code to their blogs.

Managed WordPress hosting is the hybrid of free blog platforms and traditional web hosts. You still buy space on a server computer, but you can only use the space for WordPress. You can customize WordPress the way you want, but the host manages the installation. That way you don't need to know any technical details outside of WordPress.

There are thousands of hosting options out there with no clear "best one." To simplify things, I recommend the biggest, most popular options. Though I don't mention them here, many smaller web hosts are worth your consideration. It all depends on your needs and how much you're willing to pay, but you often get what you pay for.

Idea #8: Sign up for a free blog platform

While you do give up a lot of control by using a free blog platform, you gain the advantage of ease of setup. If you are a new blogger or don't plan on blogging for money, this might be the best option for you.

WordPress (www.wordpress.com) offers a free blog hosting. It is a good choice to start with if you want to try WordPress before committing money to renting a host.

Tumblr (www.tumblr.com) is the most popular platform besides WordPress. Yahoo owns it and boasts over 300 million blogs. It is an excellent choice for casual bloggers because of its integration with social media.

Blogger (www.blogger.com) seems to have fallen somewhat in popularity over the past decade. Since Google owns both Blogger and AdSense, you can put AdSense ads on your blog. The clean composition interface makes Blogger an excellent choice if you enjoy writing.

Idea #9: Find a free niche blog platform

There also a few smaller blog platforms that cater to specific niches. I've provided a few options here. For more, you can try searching Google for "blogs for [niche]."

Penzu (www.penzu.com) provides online diaries. You can keep both public and private diaries. They keep private diaries safe with double password protection and military-strength encryption.

Edublogs (www.edublogs.org) provides blogs tailored for students, teachers, and schools. The blogs run on WordPress but have themes, features, and plugins customized for education.

DeviantArt (www.deviantart.com) is a community for artists to share their art. It lets you share your visual artwork and interact with other artists in the community.

Idea #10: Blog on social media

In many ways, social media is the next iteration of blogging. You might not think of Facebook as a blog, but it can be. Social media sites like Facebook have taken over many of the functions of blogs.

Facebook (www.facebook.com) offers a blogging feature called Facebook Notes. It works just like most other blogging software. You can create a note, add pictures, and format your text before publishing it publicly or only to your friends.

Twitter (www.twitter.com) is a microblogging service that limits each post (or tweet) to 140 characters of text. You can also add pictures, videos, and polls to your update feed.

LinkedIn (www.linkedin.com) also allows users to write and publish business-oriented articles on their platform. All you have to do to start is log in and click the "Write an article" button.

Idea #11: Traditional hosting

If you want the most control over your blog, you should choose traditional hosting. This is how it works: you first buy a shared hosting plan that can cost as little as a few dollars per month. You will receive access to a control panel where you can configure your website. From there, you can add custom domain names, install WordPress, and manage your files. You can also do advanced things like web programming or install a secure shopping cart.

GoDaddy (www.godaddy.com) is one of the world's largest hosting companies. They claim to have over 14 million customers. If you're looking for the biggest most well-known hosting company, this is it.

Bluehost (www.bluehost.com) is one of the hosts

officially endorsed by WordPress (www.wordpress. org/hosting). It is known for its low prices and reliability.

HostGator (www.hostgator.com) is another popular low-priced host. The same parent company that owns Bluehost also owns HostGator. They offer a low-cost cloud hosting service that they tout as being much faster than other comparable hosts.

Idea #12: Managed WordPress hosting

If you're planning on blogging professionally, managed WordPress hosting is your best option. It is more expensive than most of your other options, but you often get what you pay for. Since managed WordPress hosts are built specifically for WordPress, they are faster and more secure.

WPEngine (www.wpengine.com) is the most well-known managed WordPress host. Plans start at $29 per month for one WordPress installation.

FlyWheel (www.getflywheel.com) uses its smaller size to its advantage, focusing on excellent customer service and human interaction. Managed WordPress plans start at $15 per month for one installation.

SiteGround (www.siteground.com) offers one of the

cheapest managed WordPress hosting options. It has a good balance of features starting at $9.95 per month.

Idea #13: Green hosting

You might sleep more comfortably at night knowing that your website is run by wind power or other environmentally friendly energy. A few sites now offer "green hosting."

GreenGeeks (www.greengeeks.com) claims to be "300% green" and powered by renewable energy. They do it by replacing three times the amount of energy your website uses with wind power credits.

Dreamhost (www.dreamhost.com) is another one of the big players in the web hosting market. It is certified carbon neutral by various environmental groups.

FatCow (www.fatcow.com) powers all their offices and data centers with 100% wind energy.

Idea #14: Pay for a third-party blogging platform

Not all blog platforms are free. Some offer the same ease of use as free blog platforms like

Tumblr, but with premium features. Paid third-party platforms are essentially the same as managed WordPress hosts, except that they don't use WordPress.

Typepad (www.typepad.com) is based on the Movable Type platform, which predates WordPress by a few years. Plans start at $8.95 per month, and there is a free trial.

SquareSpace (www.squarespace.com) emphasizes beautiful designs. Choose from a large collection of themes, and customize them through an easy-to-use interface. Plans start at $12 per month.

Posthaven (www.posthaven.com) offers simple, easy blogs that will last forever. They promise to keep your blog running for the long haul, perhaps even 100 years from now. They also promise to keep the price at $5 a month, forever.

Idea #15: Write for the community

You don't even have to have a blog to earn a living blogging. You can write for someone else. You won't have your own blog, but you can get payment and recognition for your work.

HubPages (www.hubpages.com) is like a big shared

blog. If your articles get a lot of page views, they will share the advertisement revenue with you.

Anyone with a computer can make money online these days by freelancing. Fiverr (www.fiverr.com) and Upwork (www.upwork.com) are two sites where you can find people to pay you to write blog posts. Freelancing jobs most often don't give you public recognition, but you will get paid for them.

There are many websites that you can apply to write for. They will pay you if they use the articles you write. About.com (www.about.com) and Digital Journal (www.digitaljournal.com) are a couple of the bigger sites, but with a little searching, you can find more.

If your goal isn't to make money, but to share content and interact with readers, there are many websites that are powered by user content:

Medium (www.medium.com) is a social journalism site. Once published, articles can be upvoted by readers. The front page shows the most popular articles.

Quora (www.quora.com) is a question-and-answer site. You can ask questions, answer questions, or collaborate on editing the questions and answers.

Wattpad (www.wattpad.com) is a platform for

sharing stories. You can read stories or create your own to share with the community. Each story is presented as an e-book, complete with a cover image.

Idea #16: "Blog" on the forums

Internet forums are one of the oldest ways to publish content on the internet. They are like blogs in many ways. If you enjoy interacting with other internet users, you might enjoy joining a forum more than blogging.

Reddit (www.reddit.com) is a popular news aggregation and discussion site.

4chan (www.4chan.org) is an image-based bulletin board where users can post comments and share images.

Yahoo! Groups (groups.yahoo.com) is one of the largest forums on the internet.

Finding a great domain name

A domain name is what someone types to visit your blog. It is often the first contact the visitor has with your site, so it is important that you make a good impression. A potential reader will judge your blog by its domain name before ever visiting it.

There are a few general rules for finding a good domain name. First, it should be easy to spell and easy to say. Imagine telling someone your blog address over the phone. People know blogger Nathalie Lussier as the Real Foods Witch. She got that name by accident. Years ago, she ran a blog called Raw Food Switch. The domain name she used was www.rawfoodswitch.com. As you can imagine, everyone read that as Raw Foods Witch, so Nathalie became known as a witch. She embraced her new name as a unique brand, but you might not be so lucky. Pay attention to the different ways someone can read a web address. Be aware of how it sounds when you say it aloud. Avoid any domain names that are confusing.

Choosing a domain name is a balancing act between the clarity of a long domain name and the potential confusion of a short one. All the short domains using real words sold out a long time ago. That's why many of the shorter domains you see—like Digg.com, Flickr.com, and even Google.com—are misspelled versions of real words. They could have just as easily named their sites DigTheNews.com, FlickerPhotosOnline.com, and GoogolSearch-

Engine.com. Those names are clearer, but are almost unwieldy in length.

Domains that end in .com are the standard on the internet, so that should be your first choice. There is some debate over how important it is to get a .com domain name instead of something else like .net or .biz. I recommend looking for a .com first. Then, if the .com you want is not available, you can consider other domain extensions. Just be aware that, for most people, the inclination is to add .com behind every web address. If you choose a different extension, you might lose a lot of traffic to people accidentally visiting the .com version of your site. An infamous example is when the U.S. government set up the official website of the White House at whitehouse.gov, but did not buy the .com version. Somebody came along and set up a pornographic website mocking President Bill Clinton at whitehouse.com.

Good domain names have few letters, few words, and few syllables. The words should be memorable and have common words that go well together. Avoid adding filler words like "my" or "the" to your domain name. Be wary of putting numbers in your domain name because people may wonder whether to spell them out or not.

Make a list of 20-30 domain names to consider. Once

you have a list, the next step is to see what names are available. Go to a domain name registrar like GoDaddy (www.godaddy.com), Name.com (www.name.com), or Register.com (www.register.com). Go down your list, and search each one to see if it is available. You will find that many of your favorite domain names are no longer available, but with some luck, you will find a few that still are. Once you find one that you like and is available, go ahead and buy it.

Your registered domain also acts as a brand name. Give your blog a name corresponding to your domain name. Remember to register your blog name on every social media site you use.

There are also many tools on the internet that can help you find a good domain name. Dot-o-mator (www.dotomator.com) has an excellent tool for finding domain names. Most of the big domain name resellers also have useful search tools for finding the perfect name.

Idea #17: Find a keyword domain name

Google gives special treatment to websites with domain names that match search terms. That means if someone searches for "pet food," Google is more likely to show results where the words "pet" and "food" appear in the web address. You can use this information to your advantage. Make a list of all the keywords associated with your topic. Check the availability of different combinations of 1-3 of those keywords in domain names.

Find a word in the dictionary that hasn't been taken yet. All the short words are taken, but you might find an available word if it is a longer or more obscure word. You can also try different extensions other than .com. Some examples of dictionary word domain names include Amazon.com, Yahoo.com, and Twitter.com.

Put two or three words together in different combinations to make compound words. Doing this makes it more likely that your domain name will be available. For example, the words "desk," "author," and "pen" can be combined in 12 different ways: deskauthor.com, deskpen.com, deskauthorpen.com, deskpenauthor.com, authordesk.com, authorpen.com, authordeskpen.com, authorpendesk.com, pendesk.com, penauthor.com, pendeskauthor.com, and penauthordesk.com.

Add a trendy word to a keyword to create a memorable brand name. Some possibilities include the words zen, ninja, mastery, zip, and alpha. If your topic is parenting, you might consider the following domain names: zenparents.com, parentingninja.com, parentingmastery.com, zipdad.com, or alphamom.com.

Idea #18: Make up a portmanteau

A portmanteau is a blend of parts of words to create a new word. Wikipedia, Instagram, Microsoft, and Comcast are all portmanteau words.

Choose two words that are associated with your topic. Say those two words together as fast as you can, ten times. Then think about how you might shorten those two words into one word to make it easier to say. For example, you might decide to shorten "plumber directory" to "plumdirect." PlumDirect.com is a much better domain name than PlumberDirectory.com.

Choose two or more words associated with your topic, but use only the first letter of one of the words. For example, "electronic tourist maps" can become etouristmaps.com.

Certain word endings always bring specific words to mind. When you see -opedia, you immediately think encyclopedia. When you see -osaur, you immediately think of dinosaurs. If there is a specific thought you want to invoke when someone sees your brand name, you can use this to your advantage. Want people to think of your chess blog as a definitive resource? Call it chessopedia.com. Want people to imagine a massive lumbering dinosaur when they visit your sriracha sauce fan blog? Call it srirachasaurus.com.

Idea #19: Make up a nonsense word

Pretty much every dictionary word is taken in the .com space. Because of that, companies have been exploring the next frontier of finding nonsense words. When making a nonsense word domain, just keep in mind that it needs to be easy to spell, as few syllables as possible, and easy to remember. The perfect example is Bing.com. Other examples include Diply, Zillow, and Etsy.

Think of a word associated with your topic and change one letter. RubberDuck.com may be taken, but you can always try WubberDuck.com.

Can you think of a nonsense word or sound that you enjoy saying? See if the domain names are available. Zazoosh! BamPow! Ratatatatat!

Change the ending of a topic keyword to make it

sound cute or clever. Aviator.com becomes Aviaturr.com. Magazines.com becomes Magazinely.com.

Idea #20: Come up with an initialism

There are still some relatively short domain names available. The trouble is, most of those names don't have vowels. The names without vowels often fail the pronunciation test. Fear not! You can use initialisms to put them to use.

Initialisms are abbreviations consisting of first letters. International Business Machines becomes IBM. Internet Movie Database becomes IMDb. America Online becomes AOL. Every combination of three- and four-letter .com domains is now taken. You might still be able to find a good five-letter .com domain since there are 11,881,376 possible combinations.

If your blog's name has five or more words, it is a great candidate for an initialism. Simply take the first letter of each word and string them together.

You don't actually need five or more words in your blog's name to make an initialism out of it. Just look at Internet Movie Database. It only has three words, but they used two letters to represent the word database. You can get away with this if your name has compound words. Now your Antidisestablishmentarianism Political Society blog can have a nice, short domain name: adeps.com.

You can also work backward. The military is fond of this technique of naming things. Find an available domain name, then choose words to fit the initialism. For example, I noticed abidg.com is available. How can I use that domain for my dog-grooming blog? Maybe I should call my blog Another Big Idea Dog Grooming?

Idea #21: Play with your words

Google is a made-up word that is based on another word. The word "googol" means a one followed by a hundred zeroes. It is an intentional misspelling of an obscure word. When you're coming up with a domain name, you can also play with your topic keywords to come up with some clever misspellings.

Think of a word related to your blog topic, and come up with a nonsense spelling of the word. For example, Reddit is a play on the phrase "read it," as in, "I read it on Reddit."

Misspell your topic word so that it's still pronounced the same. For example, the popular image-sharing community Imgur is a misspelling of "imager."

Sometimes when you put two words together, they can be read in more than one way. Petsmart.com is one example. Is it "Pets Mart" or "Pet Smart"? It actually doesn't matter. Either way, the name invokes ideas that are consistent with the brand.

Idea #22: Use an existing name

One of the easiest ways to find a name for your blog is to use an existing name. The advantage of using an existing name is that it is already known and has some connotations associated with it.

Use your own name. This is especially easy if you have a relatively unique name. Hello, my name is Steve Alvest. I registered SteveAlvest.com, but Alvest.com was taken.

Use a famous person's name. Some names have brand power associated with them. Buddha. Caesar. Elvis. Those names all bring certain personalities to mind. For example, when you hear someone mention Hemingway, you probably think of the writer Ernest Hemingway. HemingwayApp.com is an editing app.

Places also have brand power. Taj Mahal. Sahara. New York. When you think of those places, images come to mind. Amazon.com is named after the

Amazon River to suggest the massive scale of the store.

Idea #23: Add to the domain name

If the domain name you want is taken, sometimes you can tweak it a little to find a version that is available.

You can add prefixes or suffixes like -blog or -site. Engadget.com added the en- prefix. Friendster.com added the -ster suffix. You can also add an article like the- (theoatmeal.com) or a- (alistapart.com). Sometimes, it makes sense to make a word plural, like W3Schools.com. Other times, it might be appropriate to add a superlative like best- or fastest-, like BestBuy.com. If you get creative, you can also find words to attach to your name like -mastery, -guy, -girl, -method, -system, -information, smart-, or -hacking.

Idea #24: Buy an alternative TLD

A TLD is a "top level domain." They are the extensions at the end of your domain names, like .com, .net, or .org. There are now hundreds to choose from. Search Wikipedia for "list of top-level internet domains" to find a constantly updated list of TLDs.

Every country in the world is assigned a TLD. They are controlled by the individual countries, so some of them can be hard to acquire. Domain Hacks (www.xona.com/domainhacks) has a tool that helps you find clever uses of country TLDs. For example, www.coach.me is a habit-building site that uses the country extension for Montenegro in its domain name.

Label your name with one of the newer TLDs like .blog, .app, or .club. If your blog is called "Jim's Woodworking Blog," you might be able to get jims.-woodworking.blog as your domain name.

Use lesser-known extensions to get short domain names. One advantage of having so many TLDs is that you can once again find short domain names. All .com domain names with four or fewer letters are already taken, but you can still find them if you choose a different TLD. For example, after a quick search on GoDaddy, I found kaz.uk available for $6.99.

Idea #25: Buy a domain name from a reseller

If you have some extra money to spend and can't

find a good domain name, it may be easier just to go out and buy one. An industry has sprung up around buying domain names and reselling them at higher prices. You will find that some of the resold domain names are still quite affordable.

Some places where you can buy domain names from resellers include Flippa (www.flippa.com), GoDaddy (www.godaddy.com), and Sedo (www.sedo.com). The prices of resold domain names vary according to demand. They can range from a few dollars to hundreds of thousands of dollars.

Chapter 3

IDEAS FOR SETTING UP
YOUR BLOG

I didn't pay much attention to plugins when I first started blogging with WordPress. Then I started getting comment spam. It began as a trickle touting insurance, male enhancement, and gambling. Then it became an unmanageable torrent of comment spam. Hackers attacked my site with scripting and brute force password attacks. That's when I realized that WordPress alone is not enough. You needed some plugins.

Plugins are like apps for your blog. You install a plugin to your blog to add extra functionality. They can add security, features, and design enhancements to your blog.

WordPress makes it easy to find and install plugins. All you have to do is log in and click "Plugins" on the sidebar menu. It will show you every plugin you have installed. Find new plugins to install by clicking the "Add New" button. Doing so will take you to a page where you can browse or search for plugins. Installing a new plugin is as easy as clicking the "Install Now" button. This chapter will give you ideas on which plugins you should install.

This chapter will also give you some ideas for features you can consider adding to your blog. Features don't have to be plugins. A few standard blog features include contact pages, resource listings, and privacy policies. Many readers expect every blog to have certain sections. Consider including the ideas in this chapter into your blog.

The average user judges a website within seconds of arriving on it. You need to set up your blog so that it is appealing to readers. Readers should know what kind of blog you have at first sight. If you keep them guessing for too long, they will lose interest and wander away. Design the blog so it is easy for readers to find information. This chapter will show you some ideas for grabbing your readers' attention.

Install these plugins

Perhaps the greatest thing about WordPress is its customizability. You can install plugins to make your blog do almost anything.

A plugin is a piece of software that you can install into your blog to give it some extra functionality. Many plugins are free, but you have to pay for some of them. WordPress has a vast library of plugins that you can browse and install.

What makes WordPress so powerful is the large number of plugins it has. Adding plugins adds custom coding to your blog to make it do things above and beyond what WordPress itself can do.

Installing too many plugins can slow down your site, so you should install them on an as-needed basis. Here are some ideas.

Idea #26: Provide a way for readers to contact you

You probably don't want your personal e-mail address out there for spammers to grab. One solution is to put a contact form on your blog. That way, readers can fill out the form, and you will get emailed when they hit "Submit." Three good options to try are Contact Form 7 (www.wordpress.org/plugins/contact-form-7), Contact Form (www.wordpress.org/plugins/contact-form-maker), and

NM Contact Forms (www.wordpress.org/plugins/nm-contact-forms).

Idea #27: Add social media buttons to your blog

You can increase the chances for your blog posts to go viral by adding social media buttons. This makes it easy for readers to share your article on social media sites. Some excellent options include AddToAny Share Buttons (www.wordpress.org/plugins/add-to-any), Simple Share Buttons Adder (www.wordpress.org/plugins/simple-share-buttons-adder), and MashShare Social Media Share Buttons (www.wordpress.org/plugins/mashsharer).

Idea #28: Optimize your blog with these plugins

If you run a content-rich blog, your main source of traffic probably comes from search engines like Google. There are simple tricks to help Google find your site and rank it higher. To make search engine optimization easy, you should consider All-In-One SEO Pack (www.wordpress.org/plugins/all-in-one-seo-pack) or Yoast SEO (www.yoast.com/wordpress/plugins/seo/). Another tool, Google XML Sitemap Generator (www.wordpress.org/plugins/google-sitemap-generator), generates sitemaps that you can submit to Google Webmaster Tools (www.google.com/webmasters/tools) to help Google index your blog.

Idea #29: Take control of your advertisements

The easiest way you can make money on your blog is to put advertisements on it using a plugin. A few popular options are WP QUADS AdSense Integration (www.wordpress.org/plugins/quick-adsense-reloaded), AdRotate (www.wordpress.org/plugins/adrotate), and Amazon Auto Links (www.wordpress.org/plugins/amazon-auto-links).

Idea #30: Optimize page-loading times

People have short attention spans on the internet. If your blog takes longer than a few seconds to load, many of your first-time visitors will click out and never return. There are a few tricks you can use to make your blog load faster. W3 Total Cache (www.wordpress.org/plugins/w3-total-cache), WP Super Cache (www.wordpress.org/plugins/wp-super-cache), and Autoptimize (www.wordpress.org/plugins/autoptimize) are popular plugins that cache and compress your blog files for faster loading times.

. . .

Idea #31: Keep your blog safe

Just like the real world, the internet is not always a safe place. There are a lot of bad people out there who want to break into your blog, spam you, and con you out of your money. There are some plugins that can help keep you safe.

Askimet comes with all WordPress installations. You will want to enable it. Askimet filters most of your comment spam into the trash so you'll never see it.

UpdraftPlus WordPress Backup Plugin (www. wordpress.org/plugins/updraftplus) is one of the most popular WordPress backup tools. The free version lets you back up your blog once a week. You can pay for more options.

Some hackers use brute force software to try to guess your blog's password. They'll try to log in thousands of times with different passwords. WP Limit Login Attempts (www.wordpress.org/plugins/wp-limit-login-attempts) will stop brute force software in its tracks.

Idea #32: Try Jetpack

Add the power of the WordPress cloud to your blog. WordPress offers a full suite of useful tools with just one plugin. Jetpack (www.wordpress.org/plugins/jetpack) has tools for increasing your traffic, improving security, loading your page faster, and much more.

Functions your blog should have

There is some content that people have come to expect to find in any blog. Whenever I come across a blog and have no idea what it's about, I immediately look for the "About" page. If I want to contact the owner of a website, I look for the "Contact" page. These are standard pages that every website and blog should have. Here are some standard functions your blog should have, as well as some optional ones to consider.

Idea #33: Write an About page

When people visit your blog, one of the first questions they have is, "What is this?" It's a good idea to have a page explaining what your blog is and who you are. This is a great place to elaborate on your blog's hook. Write a little about yourself. It also helps to build rapport with readers if you include photographs of yourself.

Readers might also want to know a little bit about where you're blogging from. Write about your location. What city or country do you live in? What does your work area look like? If you have a company, what does the building look like? What are some neat things about the area where you live?

If a visitor to your blog wants to contact you, what is the best way? In your Contact page, you should include the preferred methods of contacting you. You might include your e-mail and address. If that's too personal to put out there, you can consider including a contact form that hides your email address.

Idea #34: Write a Now page

Derek Sivers is known for starting the online music store CD Baby. He advocates bloggers including Now pages in their blogs (www.sivers.org/nowff). A Now page is a page describing what you're currently working on. Whenever a reader is wondering what you're up to, they can visit the Now page to find out.

Idea #35: Write a Purpose page

A company called Fictive Kin (www.fictivekin.com)

advocates creating Purpose pages (www. slashpurpose.org). A Purpose page is where you write about your vision for the future. Readers can visit the page to find out what the purpose of your blog is.

Idea #36: Include legal disclosures

Bloggers are expected to follow the same rules that businesses follow, especially when there is money involved. If you live in the United States, you should search "FTC blogger guidelines" on your favorite search engine, and read some of the things the FTC has to say. The short version is this: if you make money from any endorsements or include any affiliate links on your blog, you need to disclose that to your readers.

It is also a good idea to have a privacy policy. Let readers know if you collect any information from them, and what you do with that information. I am not a lawyer, so I can't advise you on how to write one, but you can do some searching online for examples. In his book, *How to Make Money Blogging*, Bob Lotich offers his privacy policy as an example to provide inspiration (www.christianpf.com/privacy-policy). He also suspects that Google rewards websites that include a privacy policy.

. . .

Idea #37: Make your blog mobile-friendly

As the popularity of mobile devices increases, you can expect more people to read your blog from their phones and tablets. The screens on those devices may be tiny. To avoid turning off those potential readers, you should make sure your blog is mobile-friendly. Gather all your mobile devices, and look at your website on each one. Make sure your text is easy to read. Test your menus to ensure easy navigation. See if your advertisements render correctly. Try to read your blog as a member of your audience would. If it's the first time you've ever seen your blog on a mobile device, you may be in for a surprise.

Idea #38: Set your permalinks

Permalinks are the web addresses leading to each blog post. In your WordPress settings, you have the option to set different styles of permalinks. You can include the category, the date, ID numbers, or titles in the permalinks. From a search-engine-optimization standpoint, you should set your permalinks to include only your post titles, and maybe the category. Most search engines put a lot of weight on the words appearing in the web address. By including your post titles and categories in your permalinks, you ensure that the relevant keywords will be in the web address for each article.

If your content is time-dependent, you can consider including the date. Using an ID number in your permalink is not advisable, but it may be useful in some cases where you want a shorter, simpler web address.

Why you need a pretty blog

New users make a judgment of your site within a second of visiting. First impressions matter. A lot. You need the initial view of your page to look as appealing as possible to the reader.

There is a statistic called a "bounce rate." That is the percentage of people who visit your blog, then leave without looking at anything else. These are those people who are looking for something and don't see it when they click into your site. You want the bounce rate to be as low as possible. You want as many people as possible to visit your site and get sucked in to look at what else you have. A great design is the key.

. . .

Idea #39: Design your blog on paper

Your blog design should be simple and clean. If you're starting from scratch, the first thing you need to do is organize your information. Get a sheet of paper, and write down all the topics your blog will cover. Then write down everything that will go on your blog, including content, links, advertisements, and images. Draw a big rectangular box on a separate sheet of paper. That is your computer screen. Draw how you envision your website in that box.

Sketch where the menus will be and any navigation elements. Draw how each post should be displayed, as well as how the most recent posts should be featured. Think about where advertisements and other sections might be placed. Doing this will help you choose the right theme for your site. If you are paying a designer, this sketch will also help them in the design process.

Idea #40: Provide directional cues

Readers are more impressionable than you might imagine. What was the first word on this page? Chances are, I just made you look at the top of the page. If you want your readers to take a certain action, tell them so. Highlight buttons you want them to click. Provide directional cues like arrows to guide the eye. Use white space to draw attention to certain elements. Establish a clear visual hierarchy of the order a reader should look at things.

Here's a trick: if you have a picture of a person on your page, readers are likely to look wherever the pictured person is looking.

Here's another trick: put an image at the top of a blog post and align it right or left. Let your first lines of text be squished between the picture and the side of the page. Doing this will accelerate the reader from the opening words of your blog post down into the meat of your article.

Get in the habit of analyzing any article that drew you in, or sales page that compelled you to buy. Why did you read the entire article? What is the structure of the beginning of the article? Why did you click the "Buy" button on that sales page?

Idea #41: Try some Photoshop alternatives

Adobe Photoshop is the industry standard for image editing, but it's expensive, and many people don't want to invest the money in it. Luckily, there are many great free alternatives out there. Canva (www. canva.com), PicMonkey (www.picmonkey.com), and iPiccy (www.ipiccy.com) have sophisticated cloud-based image editing. No software download required. If you don't mind downloading software, Paint.NET (www.getpaint.net) and GIMP (www.gimp.org) are free alternatives to Adobe Photoshop. They might not be as powerful, but they will do the job for most users.

Idea #42: Find the perfect theme

Besides content, the most important thing that will differentiate your blog from every other blog is its theme. A theme is a collection of files that define what your blog looks like and how it behaves. You can change the way your blog looks by changing its theme. There are many free themes that you can download and install on your blog. WordPress has a massive library of free themes.

If you're serious about differentiating your blog, you should consider paying for a theme. WordPress provides a directory of premium theme designers (www.wordpress.org/themes/commercial). A couple of other places to check out are ThemeForest (www.themeforest.com) and WP Hub (www.wphub.com).

You should also consider buying a theme frame-work. A theme framework is a basic theme that you can install other themes on top of. You first install the framework, then you can install various customizations called "child themes" on top of it. Some popular ones include Genesis (www.studiopress.com), Thesis (www.diythemes.com), and Storefront (www.woocommerce.com).

Another option is to hire a designer. This option costs more money, but it will give you a blog theme that closely aligns with the specific vision of what you want your blog to look like. Upwork (www.upwork.com) is a good place to find a freelance web designer to customize your website. You can also try a crowd-based design company like 99designs (www.99designs.com) or DesignCrowd (www.designcrowd.com).

Idea #43: Test your blog's usability

Have someone who has never seen your blog before sit down and look at it for a few minutes. Were there any parts where the reader hesitated or found confusing? Did she make any mistakes? Remember: there is no such thing as a user mistake. If the user made a mistake, you have a problem with your user interface. Did your reader have any questions where the answer wasn't obvious? You will need to address those.

If you don't have a friend around, you can also do user testing virtually. Peek (peek.usertesting.com) is a free user-testing service. When you enter your site's address and email address, they will send you a five-minute video of someone using your blog for the first time.

A more sophisticated way to test your blog is to run an A/B test. This is where you show half of your visitors one version of your website, and the other half another version. Then you can see which version gets the best response. You can do this by hand, but it is a cumbersome process. There is also software that helps automate and speed things up. A couple of popular options are Optimizely (www.optimizely.com) and Visual Website Optimizer (www.vwo.com).

Chapter 4

IDEAS FOR RUNNING YOUR BLOG

Consistency is key to being a professional. You need to show up and clock in every single work day. If you stop showing up to work, your readers will abandon you. The first part of this chapter will give some ideas on how to build a consistent writing habit.

The second section of the chapter will give some tips for crafting blog posts. There are some tricks and best practices you should know when writing blog posts. Follow the guidelines in this part to write blog posts that your readers will enjoy reading.

The final section of this chapter discusses how to run your blog like a business. The goal of your blog doesn't have to be about money. But if you run your blog like a business, you will come across to readers as more professional. Readers will come to respect what you say more if you are professional.

Building a writing habit

Building a daily writing habit is crucial to long-term blogging success. Write a little every day, even if it's only a paragraph. It helps to set aside a specific time every day when you will write in your blog. Make it as early in your day as possible, before the day's stresses tire you out and you find excuses not to do it.

Keep a regular posting schedule, and stick with it. Readers like to know when they can expect to see new content. If your blog doesn't have a consistent posting schedule, your readers will soon tire of checking your blog for updates and not finding any. An inconsistent blog will have inconsistent readers.

Work extra hard and build up a backlog of posts during the first few months. A backlog of draft posts will ensure that you can stick with the schedule even when you go on vacation or have unexpected things happen. And unexpected things will happen. Having a pile of draft posts ready to publish will help keep you consistent and reduce stress.

Here are some more ideas for building a writing habit and staying consistent.

Idea #44: Use the Pomodoro Technique

The Pomodoro Technique (www. pomodorotechnique.com) is a time-management technique developed by Francesco Cirillo in the late 1980s. The idea is that you work for 25 minutes of focused work, followed by a five-minute rest. Each 25-minute sprint of work is called a Pomodoro. After every four Pomodoros, take a 30-minute break. During the breaks, you can do anything to rest—anything except work. Get up and walk around, use the restroom, get a cup of coffee, do some exercises, meditate, whatever.

Idea #45: Have a Miracle Morning

In his book The Miracle Morning, Hal Elrod outlines a morning routine that changed his life and made him more productive. He sums it up with the acronym S.A.V.E.R.S., which stands for Silence, Affirmations, Visualization, Exercise, Reading, and Scribing.

Start by waking up an hour earlier than you

normally do. In that extra hour, go through all six parts of S.A.V.E.R.S. in any order you like. Silence means doing meditation, prayer, or just sitting in silence for a few minutes. For Affirmations, you should say positive things to yourself to get into a good mindset. Visualization is imagining yourself succeeding in your day. Get the blood flowing for the Exercise portion. It can be as simple as doing some stretches, or as intense as doing 15 minutes of CrossFit exercises. For the Reading portion, read something useful or inspirational for at least 10 minutes. Finally, Scribing is just a fancy way of saying writing. Spend 10 minutes writing something. It can be anything.

Idea #46: Plan ahead

Any daily plan can get derailed by unforeseen circumstances. That's why it's important to schedule blocks of time for writing blog posts. Write as many blog posts as possible during your writing time. Don't post all of them. Schedule them for the future, or save them in your drafts. You need to build a buffer so that when things pop up to mess with your day, your blog will still keep humming along.

Consistency is important to building an audience for your blog. Readers will not come back to your blog regularly if you don't post regularly. You should set a schedule for when you post, and stick to it.

How frequently you post can also be one of the main features of your blog. Readers like knowing precisely when new content will be posted. You can post daily, weekly, or monthly. You can even post more irregularly, like "four times a week" or "every 9 AM and 9 PM." Then you can advertise your frequency of posting in your blog hook. "I'll teach you how to get started with a new skill every week," "Monthly restaurant review newsletter," or "Stock market news every day at the closing bell."

One tool for consistent posting is the editorial calendar. Plan all the content you will be releasing several months in advance. Then when you write your posts, you always know what you will write next. Having an editorial calendar also allows you to work ahead.

How frequently you post depends on the depth of your content. If it is short content with only a few sentences, it is best to post daily or even several times a day. If your content is long-form content that takes hours of painstaking research to complete, once a week or even once every couple weeks is sufficient. The advantage of posting less frequently is that it allows more time for readers to comment on each post, and gives you more time to focus on quality.

~

Writing blog posts

The most important element of a good blog post is compelling content. Readers need a good reason for spending time reading your blog. They have to learn something new, be entertained, or find the information they were looking for. Your priority should always be to write great content.

Once you have great content to provide to your readers, you can learn a few tricks to craft the content into engaging blog posts that your audience will want to read. This section has ideas for how to write great blog posts. Read through the ideas, and make a checklist of the most useful and interesting ones. Then, every time you write a blog post, go through your list and make sure you hit all the points.

Idea #47: Know your audience

When writing blog posts, it helps to know who your audience is. What kinds of people read your blog? It may help to profile a few fictitious readers who represent your audience. Write down each character's traits, what they do for a living, and what problems they have. Name them something memorable. For example, you might come up with Blogger Betty as one of your typical readers. She is a suburban mom of two small children who works in an office during the day. At night, after the kids go to bed, she stays up for an extra hour to write blog posts.

Whenever you write in your blog, picture your readers looking at your articles. Try to solve their problems. Speak to them.

Idea #48: Blog on the go

Most bloggers sit at their computer and write out blog posts. Many blog platforms let you email in posts. That means you can easily post to your blog from your smartphone on the go. This is well suited for "live blogging" as things are happening, or sending out short updates while you are doing something. The idea is like Twitter, but you can do this on your blog, too. In WordPress, you can set this up by going to your Settings and enabling "Post via email."

Idea #49: Rock your headlines

Advertising pioneer John Caples has said that the most effective headlines have at least one of four qualities: self-interest, news, curiosity, and a quick, easy way. Self-interest headlines are like, "Get the first month free." News headlines go, "New law means you pay 30% less." A curiosity headline looks like, "This ancient Egyptian trick stops hair loss." Quick, easy-way headlines go like, "Save $100 with just one click!"

Pay attention to any headline that grabs your attention. Keep a file of them. Whenever you see an eye-popping headline, make a clipping and add it to your file. Go to your favorite news sites and look at what headlines get the most attention from readers. Pay attention to the headline structures of the most popular articles. Why do people click on them?

Try plugging your headline into an automated headline analyzer to get some tips on how you can improve it. The CoSchedule Headline Analyzer (www.coschedule.com/headline-analyzer) and Emotional Marketing Value Headline Analyzer (www.aminstitute.com/headline) will show you the strengths and weaknesses of your headlines, and offer tips on how to improve it.

Idea #50: Write a strong lede

In any blog post, the first sentence is your lede, and it is the most important one in your post. It needs to summon enough reader curiosity that they can't leave without reading the next sentence. By then, you want to have the reader hooked.

Bestselling author James Altucher says you should always bleed a little on the first line. He means this both figuratively and literally. If you can start your article with blood, readers will be drawn into the story. Why was the author bleeding out of her ears? Readers will want to know.

Another bestselling author, Tim Ferriss, says he learned a formula from a Wired writer. Make the first paragraph involve a specific person. It can be a question, a situation, or something the person said. Make the second paragraph a "nutgraph," where you explain the topic of the post. You can describe the underlying trend and statistics to back it up. Then close the paragraph with the "nut," explaining what you'll teach the reader in the rest of the article.

Another strategy is to make your first few paragraphs very short. They can even be single sentences. It makes the beginning of your article quick to read, and readers naturally flow into reading the rest of the article.

. . .

Idea #51: Write good structure

When you're writing a blog post, think of your article as a list. Do this even if your article is not a list. It is useful to think of it as a list because it injects structure into your thinking while you're writing. You will find that the words come easier when you have a sequential outline to work from.

Blog readers tend to scan articles. The torrent of new blog posts comes too fast for most readers, and they need to make quick decisions about whether a new article is worth reading or not. Make it easy for readers to make the decision. Make your posts scannable. That means including lots of subheadings. Break big paragraphs up into single lines. Bold or italicize text to emphasize important points. Add quotes, graphics, and whitespace.

James Altucher suggests deleting your first and last paragraphs after you're done writing. He says this works even if you know you're going to do it while you're writing. Try it. See if it makes your article more compelling. It often does, by removing needless explanation.

You want to end your articles strong. Be sure to end them with a takeaway, call to action, or witty line that makes the readers think.

. . .

Idea #52: Try a robot editor

While there is no replacement for a good human editor, automated editing services can catch many of the grammatical errors in your articles. All you have to do is paste your writing into the editor, and it will analyze it for common grammatical mistakes. Some of the more popular ones include Hemingway (www. hemingwayapp.com), Grammarly (www. grammarly.com), and After the Deadline (www. polishmywriting.com).

Idea #53: Make your blog posts visual

Besides writing, one of the most important skills for a blogger to have is photography. You should get a good camera and learn to use it. These days, most premium smartphones have very good cameras. Other than the camera, the other thing you need for taking excellent photographs is good lighting. When you take a picture, make sure there is nothing distracting in the background. Use the "Rule of Thirds." Imagine the view with grid lines similar to tic-tac-toe. You want to get the focal point of your picture on one of the lines or intersections. To learn more, try taking a course on photography. There are many you can take online.

If you don't want to take the pictures yourself, at least get them from somewhere else. There are many places online where you can find royalty-free pictures. This is important. Don't take pictures from other people unless they give you permission or you can confirm that they are royalty-free. Even if they are royalty-free, you almost always need to credit the source. Unsplash (www.unsplash.com) is one of the few websites that don't require you even to credit the source. Foter (www.foter.com) and Flickr (www.flickr.com) each have hundreds of millions of pictures that you can search through. Many of the images are free to use if you attribute the source. Just make sure the pictures allow commercial use if you are making any money from your blog (including advertisements).

Idea #54: Refresh your old content

Darren Rowse of ProBlogger.net goes through a process for refreshing old blog content every day. He determines what day it was six months ago. Then he goes back to all his past blog posts from the current day and the day six months ago, reviews them, and updates them. For example, if today is September 12, you count back six months to March 12. Then you go through all your previous blog posts that were posted on September 12 or March 12 and update them. When you update, look for any errors that need to be fixed. Do you need to include a new call to action? Do all the links still work? Or maybe the post is no longer relevant and should be deleted. Should you promote the post on social media? If you follow this process, you will be sure that every post on your blog gets updated every six months.

An approach I like to take with my own blog is to think of my posts as arranged in a circle. Whenever it is time to post another article, I either write a new post, or update an old post and repost it as new. This way I have a never-ending cycle of blog posts, and I can post daily without ever running out.

$$\sim$$

Blogging like a business

If you plan to make money from your blog, you should treat your blog like a business. Approach your blog with the same discipline as you do your job.

Since most bloggers work from home, the biggest challenge is to approach blogging professionally. It's too easy to spend your afternoons playing with your kids, running errands, or hanging out when you should be working. The home has a lot of distractions. There is no boss breathing down your neck and asking when your next post will be written. You need to set your own hours and discipline yourself.

Here are some ideas for putting some discipline into your blogging and becoming more productive.

Idea #55: Make your blog an official business

If you make any significant income from blogging, you should consider organizing it as an official business. That means you register your blog as an official business with your local government. I am not a lawyer, and laws change all the time, so you need to verify suggestions provided here with a licensed attorney.

One common practice in the United States is to start a Limited Liability Corporation, or LLC. This sets you up to make money and pay taxes. It also provides the benefit of reducing your liability in case someone decides to sue you.

If you make over $50,000 from your blog, you should look into organizing as an S-Corp. Again, I am not a lawyer, but I've heard there may be tax benefits for doing so.

For organizing your own LLC or S-Corp, you can consider services like LegalZoom (www. legalzoom.com) or RocketLawyer (www. rocketlawyer.com). These are services that turn legal processes like organizing a corporation into easy step-by-step processes that you can do online.

Another thing to look into is getting a Tax ID or Employer Identification Number (EIN). Doing this will allow you to avoid using your social security number when you sign up for advertising or affiliate networks.

Idea #56: Get a P.O. or UPS box

You might want to consider renting a post office or UPS box for your blog business. If you use your home address online, you may get unwanted visitors. Use a P.O. Box or UPS address whenever possible to hide your home address. If you decide to create a mailing list, you will need to provide an address. You might be uncomfortable sending your home address to thousands of mailing list subscribers.

Idea #57: Create a business plan

Even if your blog business doesn't have any partners

or employees, it is useful to have a mission statement and business plan. These provide a big-picture plan to guide you in making major decisions for your blog.

A mission statement is a succinct paragraph that sums up what your company is trying to accomplish. It includes a statement of core values, which are the beliefs that you want your business to represent.

A business plan can be a few paragraphs describing the goals of your blog business. What are you trying to accomplish with your blog? How do you plan on making money? Do you have an end goal? What happens when you achieve that goal? Do you have an exit strategy in case you decide to do something else a few years down the line? What are some concrete goals you have, both short-term and long-term?

It is also useful to identify your audience. What type of person visits your blog? What is the background of the average visitor of your blog? This information is invaluable when you are writing blog posts or marketing to your audience.

Idea #58: Set monthly goals

Challenge yourself to stay motivated. One way is to

set monthly goals. These are short-term goals that break your long-term goals down into manageable chunks. They help focus your priorities.

One month is an ideal amount of time for a goal. It is just long enough for you to accomplish something big, but short enough so that if the project fails you can move on to a new project quickly. You can accomplish a lot in a year by setting 12 monthly goals.

Idea #59: Track your numbers

Business management consultant Peter Drucker once said, "What gets measured, gets managed." It is important to keep track of certain metrics for your blog. That is the only way you can know if you're making progress or wasting your time.

One thing you can do is install Google Analytics (www.google.com/analytics). It can be intimidating with all the data you can track, so you should keep it simple. I suggest tracking total unique visitors, total visitors from your top 10 traffic sources, and average visitor duration. Enter these numbers into a spreadsheet, and try to look at them only once a month. You can easily waste a lot of time analyzing your statistics when you should be blogging. Some other analytics tools you can consider are StatCounter (www.statcounter.com), SiteMeter (www.sitemeter.com), and Adobe Analytics (www.adobe.com/analytics). There are also many WordPress plugins you can install that will show you analytics data directly from your blog interface.

If you run a commercial blog, you should also track expenses and revenue related to your blog. At the very least, write down each expense you incur and each check you receive as a result of your blogging efforts. This information is useful when tax time comes. It is also useful to know if you are making money or losing money from blogging.

Another thing you can track is people you interact with. With all the blogs you might follow and all your email and social media interactions, it can be easy to forget things. Keep a spreadsheet of all your interactions with other people related to your blog. That way, it will be easier to keep track of every promise you make, every favor you asked, and which contacts you should follow up on.

Idea #60: Build your team

As your blog grows, you may find it worthwhile to delegate certain tasks to others. Some tasks that can be delegated include administrative work, copy editing, photo editing, accounting, design, advertising, public relations, and legal assistance. You should consider delegating whatever you're not that good at, and whatever you don't like to do yourself.

Two of the most popular places to hire help online are Freelancer (www.freelancer.com) and UpWork (www.upwork.com). Both sites help match prospective employers with freelancers. All you have to do is post a detailed description of the work you need to be done, choose a freelancer to hire and work with them to get the job done. If you want to take baby steps, I recommend trying Fiverr (www.fiverr.com) where you can hire people to do small jobs for minimal investments of $5.

Chapter 5

IDEAS FOR BLOG POSTS

B y now, your blog is set up. You've made all the most important decisions. It looks good and runs well. You have a consistent professional writing habit. Writer's block creeps in for many people at this point. They might have had some great ideas for articles in the beginning. But once they wrote and published those posts, the idea well ran dry. The result is another abandoned blog. Don't let this happen to you.

That's where this chapter comes in handy. Whenever you get writer's block, come back here and look through the ideas. This section will give you ideas for different types of blog posts, with many prompts to go with them.

I've divided the blog post ideas into three broad

categories: introspective, current events, and research. The categories are differentiated by the type of content they relate to; however, there are dozens of different types of blog posts that don't correspond to a specific type of content. Three of the most popular types are series posts, list posts, and link posts. You can pick any of the ideas in this chapter and write one of these three types of blog posts with it.

Series posts teach a huge lesson through a set of articles. You can publish the series of posts over a period of weeks, months, or even years. Series posts work well for breaking up a big topic into smaller, more readable posts. You can also use them for tracking progress for something that is ongoing. Or you can use a series to provide updates whenever you learn something new about the topic of your series.

List posts are just as the name implies. They provide lists about the topic. You can turn almost any prompt into a list post. For instance, "How to make money online" can become "7 ways to make money online." Including a specific number in the title does a better job of grabbing a reader's interest.

Finally, link posts are articles centered around one or more links. You might have read an interesting article online and want to share it with your readers.

Or maybe you want to share a bunch of links that your readers may find helpful.

Introspective blog posts

In the early days of the internet, blogs began as personal websites. The easiest source of ideas for blog posts is to look within yourself. What are your interests? What are your favorite things? What knowledge do you have to share?

Introspective blog post topics are all about you. You don't need to do any research to write about them because they are things you already know. To write about these subjects, draw on your experiences and opinions. Teach what you know. Tell people your thoughts. Tell stories of your memories and experiences.

Idea #61: Recap a mistake you made

People love hearing about other people's blunders. More importantly, they also want to know how they can avoid the same mistakes.

Prompts: My big social blunder. The worst thing I've ever done. Confessions of a _____. The biggest challenge that I've yet to overcome. My shocking bad habit. My embarrassing work story. My marketing failures.

Idea #62: Tell people what you think

Sometimes, people visit your blog to get your opinions on matters. It's easy to write your thoughts. All you have to do is find a topic and write whatever comes to mind. Writing your opinions also allows readers to get to know you better. They might find that they have a lot in common with you.

Prompts: My manifesto. The one person I couldn't live without. The thing that scares me most. The community I love most. Who I would cast for [book you've read]. If I could visit anywhere in the world, I would go here. The person I most want to have lunch with. An open letter to ____. If I could travel back in time, I would go back to ___. What it feels like to be ___. If I could choose three people to coach me, I would choose ___. What I would do this week if I knew I would die on Friday. If I were a fictional character, I would be ___. The thing that drives me crazy.

Idea #63: Tell people about your aspirations

Telling people about your goals and aspirations on your blog creates public accountability. You will be more likely to succeed in your goals if you tell everyone about them. Consider setting big goals and telling your readers about them.

Prompts: My big goal for this year. What my vision board looks like. What I want in my eulogy when I die. Places I want to go before I die. How I'm challenging myself this month. My bucket list. I'm saving up to buy ___. My plan for the next [#] years. The biggest thing I want to change in my life. The person I most want to meet.

Idea #64: Tell a story

If your readers identify with you, they will be more likely to read your blog. Tell them your story. What are the most interesting experiences you've had in your life?

Prompts: My hometown. My life before ___. Why I now live in ___. Nobody knows that I ___. The thing that drives my passion. The thing I do differently from everyone else. The achievement I'm most proud of. Why I do what I do. The best gift I've ever received. How I became ___. My first memory. The turning point in my life. How I got started doing

___. My favorite memory. What it was like when I was living in ___. The song playlist that corresponds with my life. The most difficult time in my life. How I overcame ___.

Idea #65: Write a how-to post

Everyone is good at something. Share whatever you're best at with your readers. Teach them how they can start. Teach them some of the tricks that may not be obvious.

Prompts: How I use [favorite social media]. How to use [favorite app]. How to find blogging ideas. How to do my job. Getting started with [hobby]. The technique I use every day. How I do ___ differently. The technique that contributed to my success. How I got from [low point] to [high point]. The ultimate guide to ___. How to ___. A beginner's guide to ___.

Idea #66: Provoke controversy

Depending on your personality and appetite for debate, you may or may not want to provoke controversy on your blog. It is one of the best ways to get a discussion going. Argue one side of a controversial debate. Rant about something you're angry at. Play Devil's advocate and consider why people should consider doing something that's unpopular or even taboo.

Prompts: Why we should all [something unpopular or taboo]. Why we should not [something popular]. Is [side 1] better than [side 2]? My (conspiracy) theory about what really happened at [emotional event]. My enraging experience with [a bad experience]. Why [popular concept] is completely wrong. ____ is never a waste of time. I'm taking a stand against ___. The dark side of ____. A reality check for ___. A contrarian view on ____. What everyone is thinking (but nobody is saying) about ____. My take on [controversy/debate].

Idea #67: Make a prediction

People love to predict the future, though few are actually right. It's often fun to put a prediction out there, then come back to it in the future to see if you were right.

Prompts: What will ____ be like in 100 years? The future of ___. What ___ will look like in 10 years. What will happen next year in the ____ industry? How ____ will impact ____.

~

Current event blog posts

People want to read about things that are relevant to them. One way to provide relevant information is to write about current events and trends. These are topics that are on everyone's mind. Readers are proactive in seeking out more information on these issues. Everyone is talking about them.

The news is easy to find in any country with freedom of the press. Turn on the television. Read your local newspaper. Listen to the radio. Browse some news sites online. Then write about the story you found most interesting.

When the same story keeps happening repeatedly, it becomes a trend. If you read the news every day, you will begin to notice patterns. They are easy to find online. Google Trends (www.google.com/trends) shows the latest trends based on Google searches. Twitter (www.twitter.com) also shows trending topics based on hashtags.

When writing current event blog posts, be aware that they will not be evergreen. Your content will be relevant for a limited amount of time. While it may generate a lot of traffic when you post it, the traffic fizzles fast. Your blog post will become obsolete once the topic is no longer in the news.

Idea #68: Write a profile

People like reading about other people, especially their role models. Every person has a story, and every story has lessons we can learn. You can profile historical figures, celebrities, or regular people. Why is the person interesting? What unique experiences did they have? What lessons can we learn from them? Profiles don't have to be limited to people either. You can also profile businesses, cities, or other blogs.

You can get the content for a profile through research, but it is better if you can interview someone. The advantage of interviewing someone is that the information is fresh and maybe even exclusive. You can ask questions that nobody asked before.

Prompts: A day in the life of ___. The best works of ___. Lessons I learned from ___. The best quotes from ___. How ___ became a success. Who to follow on [social network].

Idea #69: Write about lessons learned

We learn new things every day. It is just a part of living. One of the biggest reasons why people blog is to teach others the lessons they learned. Write about the lessons you learned this past week.

Prompts: What I gained (or lost) by taking a risk. My foray into [new skill]. My biggest regret. My experience as a ___. Life advice for my kids. Things I wish I knew when I was younger. What I wish I had known before I started ___. I wouldn't be where I am today without ____.

Idea #70: Write about the news

While you can't compete with the major news outlets for the raw world news, you can report on local and niche events. You can also write about the news from a different perspective and provide a deeper analysis.

One way to identify trends is to track hashtags on social media. On Twitter (www.twitter.com), trending tags are prominently displayed next to your feed. There are also premium services that help identify trending topics, such as Hashtags.org (www.hashtags.org), Trendsmap (www.trendsmap.com), and RiteTag (www.ritetag.com).

Prompts: What happened in sports yesterday. The

best stock buy of the day. A recently granted patent, and what it means for the future. My take on the ____ trend. How [news event] affects [your niche]. My thoughts on ____. The emerging trend all ____ should be aware of.

Idea #71: Write about upcoming events

Curate upcoming events that your niche audience will be interested in. They can be local events if your readers are based primarily at one location, or they can be worldwide or online events. List conferences, product launches, annual events, or special sales. Collect event information from websites like Fest 300 (www.fest300.com) or Topend Sports Major World Sporting Events (www.topendsports.com/events).

Prompts: Conferences every ____ should attend. Product launches we're waiting for. [holiday] events you should go to. The hottest concerts this year. Upcoming events you should know about.

Idea #72: Write about the day

Center your blog around the day of the year. On Christmas, write about Christmas. On Veteran's Day, write a post about Veteran's Day. You can even write about some of the lesser-known special days. Did you know that the third Sunday of August is International Homeless Animals Day? Look at Days of the Year (www.daysoftheyear.com) or Checkiday (www.checkiday.com) for inspiration.

Prompts: Did you know today is ___ Day? How I celebrate ___ Day. What you should do to observe ___ Day. My ___ Day story.

~

Research blog posts

Sometimes you don't know the information you want to write about. And it's not something new that you read about and have opinions on. You're curious about something, so you research it. Then you report to your readers the results of your research. These are research posts.

Good content is not what you think it is. If you write a helpful post about how to run a marathon that just regurgitates the same information a more popular website put online, that is not good content. Good content is something both helpful and new. Though no information is completely new—as new information builds upon a foundation of past information—

your blog posts should add at least a fresh view on the topic.

Idea #73: Write a product review

One way bloggers can provide useful information to the internet community is to write reviews. Writing about your best experiences can help others find the same experiences. Writing about bad experiences can help others avoid them.

You can review anything. Review books, movies, concerts, software, and any media imaginable. Review anything you spend money on, whether it's beverages, hotels, gadgets, or utility companies.

Writing review posts is also a great way to make money through affiliate advertising. Any time you mention a product, provide an affiliate link to that product. At the very least, you can provide an affiliate link to the products you highly recommend. That way, if someone buys it from your recommendation, you will make a commission.

Prompts: Recapping the [event, conference, or course]. A review of the most useful ____. A head-to-head comparison of ___ and ___. Should you buy a _____ or a _____? What is the best ___?

. . .

Idea #74: Hold a contest

A fun way to gain new readers and engage with existing ones is to run a contest. Challenge your audience to come up with the best photograph, the best poetry, most insightful comment, or the funniest tweet. You can draw random winners, let other readers vote, choose for yourself, or a combination.

The first step is to have a prize ready for the winner. Then you have to establish the rules of the contest. Let everyone know about the contest and the deadlines. Collect the entries and select a winner. Then you contact the winner to get shipping information and send them the prize. Finally, announce the winner on your blog.

Many places have laws against gambling, and sometimes contests can be interpreted as a form of gambling. Some places have rules against children entering contests. Be sure to look into your local laws to make sure your contest is legal.

Prompts: Photography contest. Haiku contest. Comment on this post for a chance to win. Tweet to win ___. Send in a picture of you doing [some activity] to win!

. . .

Idea #75: Write a resources post

A resources post is a type of link post. You write about all the things you personally use and enjoy. Unlike review posts, these are purely recommendations. You list only the things you enjoy most and don't mention anything you didn't enjoy.

Prompts: The things I carry with me. Blogs I read every day. Most frequently used apps on my phone. My favorite books of all time. Free e-books for learning ___. My travel packing list. Best books for learning ___. Best blogs to follow about ___. The best movies of this year. Online resources for ___. Best podcasts for ___.

Idea #76: Share tips and advice

Readers might also find your tips and advice helpful. Think about the times when others have asked for your advice. What types of advice do people ask you for most often? What topics do others think you are an expert on?

Prompts: Quick tips about ___. Ways to spark your creativity. Tips for ___. Signs you should invest in ___. Productivity tips for ___. Things about ___ that your boss wants to know. Things you shouldn't waste money on. Habits every ___ should develop.

Chapter 6

IDEAS FOR GETTING TRAFFIC

The exact number is impossible to pin down, but there are likely well over 300 million blogs on the internet. Out of those blogs, over 95% are dead zombie blogs. You can still visit these decaying and abandoned blogs. The last vestiges of an audience might even haunt some of them. Spooky, I know.

There are countless reasons why owners may have chosen to abandon a blog. But if you look at the common theme among blogs that remain active, you find that most have gained an audience. Those few successful blogs out there gained an audience because they have amazing content.

I can't think of any blog that started out as an instant success. Bloggers often believe that if they just put up great content, the blog will become a success. That is not true. Nobody will read your blog if it never pops up in front of them. You need to advertise your blog. Not in a sleazy salesperson way. But you need to get the link to your blog in front of as many people as possible. People won't know about your blog unless you tell them about it somehow.

This chapter will provide tips for how you can tell people about your blog so you can build traffic. "Traffic" is just a fancy way of referring to all the people who visit your blog. You will want to increase your traffic because you want people to visit your blog. If nobody reads your content, the time you spent writing it gets wasted.

In this chapter, you will also find tips on how to make your blog more friendly to search engines. SEO stands for Search Engine Optimization. It is about making your blog content easy to find on search engines like Google. Much of the traffic most blogs get come from Google searches. That's why SEO is so important.

Social media also provides ways you can reach your potential readers. Social media platforms like Facebook and Twitter are among the most popular sites on the internet. They are now effective ways to advertise and promote your blog. The section on using social media has tips for promoting your blog through social media.

How to get traffic

Once there is some content on your blog, you will want to find readers. A common rookie mistake is to put your content online and assume people will just start finding it. If you do that, you'll most likely hear crickets after you put your content up. You need to be proactive and work to get people to visit your blog.

Think about the last new blog you visited. How did you find it? The web address didn't just pop into your head the moment it went live. You probably found it as a link on another blog, from a search engine, or from an advertisement. Maybe you even saw it on TV or heard someone mention it. The truth is, almost all of these ways you could have found out about the new blog required some work by the blogger. Sure, you can wait until Google finds your blog and hope it ranks high enough for people to find it. But doing that is like sitting around watching TV and hoping you get rich.

. . .

Idea #77: Comment on other blogs

If you read other blogs, then you already have access to some potential traffic. All you have to do is update your profile to include your blog address and start commenting on those other blogs. If one of your comments piques enough curiosity, people will want to know who you are.

When you leave a response on a forum or someone else's blog, you often can submit a website address along with your name. Sometimes the website address is displayed with your comment. It effectively puts your link on the forum or blog.

Obviously, spammers frequently abuse the privilege. Don't be a spammer. The Law of Internet Karma says that you will get deleted, banned, and ostracized when you do this. Instead, you want to be a prolific commenter who always has something valuable to say. People will look to you for advice. They will be curious about who you are. They will click your links in search of more information.

Find out where the readers of your blog hang out when they're not at your site. It may be on other blogs. Or it may be on certain forums. Become an active reader of some of these other blogs and forums. Each day, spend a few minutes visiting some blogs and forums. Answer questions, participate and contribute. Traffic to your blog will increase as a side effect.

A tool that makes it easy to find blogs to comment on is Drop My Link (www.dropmylink.com). Just enter a keyword, and it will find relevant blogs where you can leave a comment. It is best to find blogs that are a little bit bigger than your own. It also helps to comment as early as possible after a new article is posted.

Idea #78: Help others

The internet has so much information on it that many people use it to solve their problems. You can go to popular places where people ask questions and help as many people as possible. Being helpful to others is one of the best ways to build an army of loyal readers.

Go to question-and-answer sites like Quora (www.quora.com) or Yahoo Answers (answers.yahoo.com). Create an account, and add your blog's address to your user profile. Then start answering questions. Try to answer questions related to your blog's niche. You can also answer questions you see on forums and comments.

. . .

Idea #79: Guest post

Guest posting is when you write a blog post for someone else's blog. It is a great way to introduce your content to another audience.

The first step for guest posting on a blog is to determine if the blog even accepts guest posts. Some blogs are so personal to the author that a guest post would just be awkward. Other blogs accept guest posts but have strict guidelines regarding them. Always look for the website's guest posting guidelines before offering to write a guest post.

If a blogger agrees to let you guest post, submit only your best work. A guest post will only bring new readers to your blog if you impress them with great content. Remember, you are writing to someone else's audience. Try to write in the style of the blog you are guest posting on. Try to resonate with the subtle differences in the other blog's audience.

Idea #80: Write for a print publication

You don't have to limit your activities to the internet. Print publications like local newspapers, newsletters, and magazines also have audiences. Try submitting articles or letters to your favorite newspapers, newsletters, or magazines. When you do, see if you can also have your web address or blog name listed in your byline.

Idea #81: Network with other bloggers

Network freely with your niche. Join communities in your niche, like Blog Catalog (www. blogcatalog.com), Facebook Groups (www.facebook. com/groups), or Yahoo Groups (groups.yahoo.com). There are also blog conferences that you can attend. Just search your favorite search engine for "blog conferences," and you will find hundreds of them.

When you're just starting out, it is often easiest to network with other new bloggers. You can find other newer bloggers by searching on Twitter (www. twitter.com) for phrases like "first blog post" or "launched my blog." Also, look in the comments section on blogs that you read.

If you're a bit more aggressive, you can look for other bloggers in your local area and meet them in person. Create your own conference, roundtable, or master-mind group. Meet other bloggers over coffee at your local coffee shop.

Idea #82: Advertise your blog

It's not worth it to advertise on most blogs; however, if you offer a product, you can advertise the product and use your blog as a place interested people can go to for more information.

There are many places where you can advertise. Look through the *Ideas for Monetizing* chapter for ideas. You will also need to create some advertising materials like advertisement graphics, marketing text (called "copy"), and free content (called "lead magnets").

Idea #83: Link to others

When you write blog posts, link generously to posts on other blogs. But make sure your links are in context. Linking to other blogs generates trackbacks. A trackback is a notification you get when another blog links to you. If the blog you're linking to has trackbacks enabled, that blog author will get a notification that you linked to them. Sometimes, the trackback will even display on the linked blog post. It's an easy way to get some extra attention to your blog posts.

Idea #84: Join a blog hop

A blog hop is a network of blogs. Usually, it is a collection of links posted on one site or every participating blog. Link parties are similar, though they are usually centered around a single theme. Every participating blogger tries to visit the other blogs in the network and leave comments. It is a good way to get to know other bloggers in your niche.

Idea #85: Word of mouth

Tell people about your blog. Craft your elevator pitch so when you mention your blog in conversation you can tell people what your blog is about and why they should visit.

Go through your address book and send your blog link to everyone you know. Ask for honest feedback. Get accounts on every social media site your friends are on. Share your best blog posts on your social media sites.

If blogging is your primary business, or if your blog is the best way to find information about your company, have business cards printed with your blog's address on them. Share them with everyone you meet.

Have a bumper sticker or car decal printed with your

web address. This is a great way to get neighbors and people in your local area to start reading your blog.

Idea #86: Build your list

E-mail mailing lists are the most reliable way to reach your audience. Posting on your blog or social media relies on your readers to take action and check if there is new content. But e-mail is something most people check every day. Begin collecting e-mail addresses from your readers as soon as possible. The people who join your e-mail list will have your most loyal readers among them.

You should provide an incentive for joining your e-mail list. These incentives are called lead magnets. A lead magnet can be a free e-book, special report, exclusive video, bonus content, checklist, infographic, cheat sheet, or anything else you can deliver electronically for free.

There are many e-mail list services that you can choose from. Some popular ones are MailChimp (www.mailchimp.com), Aweber (www.aweber.com), ConvertKit (www.convertkit.com), and Infusionsoft (www.infusionsoft.com).

Make it easy to subscribe to your e-mail list from your blog. You can provide something as subtle as a link on your sidebar, or as aggressive as a full-page takeover asking the reader to join. It all depends on your personality and your audience's receptiveness to being pitched. There are many plugins and software tools that can help you gather email addresses. A few to consider are HelloBar (www.hellobar.com), SumoMe (www.sumome.com), and OptinMonster (www.optinmonster.com).

SEO tips for blogs

SEO is search engine optimization. SEO is more about helping Google understand what your post is about, rather than figuring out the hottest search term. Don't worry much about the SEO. Just concentrate on writing good content. Be sure to use these ideas naturally and organically in your posts, or else Google might penalize your blog for using spammy tactics like keyword stuffing.

The biggest rule of SEO is this: whatever you do, don't get banned by Google. Don't pay for text links, publish links that have been paid for, stuff keywords, hide keywords, scrape content, or publish content that is nothing more than links. If it feels deceptive and slimy, stay away from it. If you're doing something that you think Google may think is a bit shady, use the "nofollow" tag so Google won't think the link is paid.

Idea #87: Make sure your content is evergreen

Evergreen content, like evergreen trees, stays green through the years. It is content that never gets outdated. You can revisit the blog post years later, and the content will still be helpful. It is the best type of content from an SEO standpoint.

The best evergreen content tends to be long-form content that is at least 1,000 words in length. Make sure the content has a clear takeaway and resources that readers will want to come back to reference. Also, make sure your content is unique. You want your blog post to be the only place readers can find the content all in one place.

Idea #88: Publish your content on the big sites

The biggest websites almost have a monopoly on readers. You will have to fight an uphill battle to get any significant number of regular readers to your blog. Sometimes, if you can't beat them, join them. Go to some of those big websites and put your content there. Publish your best articles on Medium (www.medium.com) and other sites that will publish your articles. Polish your headline and submit some blog posts to submission sites like Reddit (www.reddit.com), Digg (www.digg.com), or EzineArticles (www.ezinearticles.com).

You want to write quality long-form content that is at least 1,200 words. Build a network of larger sites that are willing to publish your articles. Then, whenever you write another great long-form article, submit to the sites. If you can get links back to your blog, your readership will grow.

Idea #89: Generate backlinks

A backlink is a link on another website that points to your blog. If you want your blog to rank higher in search results, you need to have as many quality backlinks as possible. There are many ways to generate backlinks. As discussed previously, publishing your content on another website is one way to do it. Another way is to comment on other blogs. Share your content through all your social media channels. Put a link to your blog in all your online profiles. Whenever you find a new way to get your link on another website, take advantage of it.

. . .

Idea #90: Load up with keywords

Another way to get your blog to rank higher in search engines is to use a lot of keywords. When it comes down to it, SEO is all about keywords. Use terminology that people use when they search on search engines. Think of what your readers would type in the search box if they wanted to find your article. Make sure you use those words in your article. You can also identify popular keywords related to your niche using Google's Keyword Planner tool (adwords.google.com/KeywordPlanner).

Use the keywords often and in strategic places. Search engines attach more weight to keywords that appear in the web address, title, and headings of your articles. Use your keywords in the beginning and end of your post content. Use keywords in and around links. Remember to fill out the descriptive ALT tags for any images you include. Also, remember to fill out the metadata for your blog posts before publishing. Just don't get overzealous in putting keywords in your article. Overdoing it is called "keyword stuffing" and can get you penalized by search engines. Keep it natural.

Using social media

Social media should complement your blog. Find out what social media sites your readers hang out at and focus your attention there. Use them to engage with your readers outside of your blog and build awareness of your brand.

With social media, quality is more important than quantity. Having 100 dedicated readers sharing and discussing your content on social media is way better than having an army of 10,000 uninterested people who followed you by accident or through marketing tricks.

When you use social media for your blog, don't just post a link whenever you have a new blog post. Make sure you offer something different from your blog. Likewise, if you're on several social media platforms, be sure to put different content on each.

Idea #91: Run Facebook ads

The advantage of running ads on Facebook is that Facebook knows a lot about its users. You can run highly targeted ads that only your most likely customers will see. To get started, you should first create a lead page on your blog or through a site like LeadPages (www.leadpages.net). The lead page will be where people get directed to when they click on your ad. On the lead page, make the call to action clear. If you want visitors to join your mailing list, tell them the benefits, and make it easy for them to sign up. Set limits on how much you spend on the ads, and let them run for a few weeks so you can assess whether they are worth it or not.

Idea #92: Make a Pinterest strategy

Some bloggers swear by Pinterest (www. pinterest.com) for building their blog's audience. Pinterest lets users maintain a virtual board where they can "pin" images with associated links. You can surf the web, and whenever you find an interesting article, recipe, or other content, you can pin it to your Pinterest board.

The key to gaining followers on Pinterest is to include at least one pinnable graphic on each blog post you write. Create tall images that are colorful and eye-catching. Put text on your images that invoke curiosity. That way, when someone pins your blog post to a Pinterest board, it shows up as a warm, inviting picture that readers will want to click.

Join as many large and active collaborative boards as you can. Build a habit of regularly pinning your best content onto those boards.

. . .

Idea #93: Develop a Facebook strategy

Facebook (www.facebook.com) is the largest social network. Creating a fan page for your blog on Facebook is an excellent way to start promoting your blog on social media. Once you create a fan page, you can make a strategy for growing your audience.

Methodically post a set number of updates every day. On Facebook, you can post photos, videos, or text. It's a good idea to mix them up. Post anything you think your readers would find valuable or entertaining. Include a mix of inspirational quotes, amusing pictures, and helpful links. You can use a scheduling app like Buffer (www.buffer.com) to post content at regular intervals. Posting a few times a day, spaced apart by a few hours, seems to work well for a lot of bloggers. Be sure to include an image with every post. You can also help grow your Facebook audience by including "Like" buttons on your blog.

Idea #94: Build your audience with LinkedIn

LinkedIn (www.linkedin.com) is a social network oriented towards business professionals. It is a great place to connect with others in your industry. With LinkedIn, you can participate in or start group discussions, interact with influencers, and share business-related articles. Start with filling out your LinkedIn profile and building your resume. Then join a few groups, and start building your network by sending invites, endorsing people you know, and soliciting endorsements. LinkedIn pages tend to rank highly in Google, so keep in mind that it might be the first page people see when they search for your name.

Idea #95: Create a Google+ profile

Google+ (plus.google.com) is the social network run by Google. Like with Facebook, you can build your following on Google+ by filling out your profile and posting content daily. Follow other people in your niche by adding them to your circles. Join some relevant communities and post comments. Join Hangouts and comment in them. Include Google+ follow buttons on your blog.

Idea #96: Building a following on Instagram

Instagram (www.instagram.com) is a photo-sharing social network owned by Facebook. You use Instagram primarily through its smartphone app. Take pictures, apply filters, and share them. Share your best, most intriguing photos. Use hashtags so others can find them easier. Be interesting and genuine, and people will want to know more about you and perhaps visit your blog.

Idea #97: Generate traffic with Twitter

Twitter (www.twitter.com) is a microblogging platform. That means each post, or tweet, must be 140 characters or less. You can also post photos, videos, and polls. As with other social media, be sure to fill out your profile and put your blog's web address on it. Tweet links to great content, pictures, and videos.

Idea #98: Use Buffer

Buffer (www.buffer.com) lets you schedule posts on social media. It works with all the major social networks. With Buffer, you don't have to waste your time posting on social networks all day. You can schedule several posts at once and have Buffer post them at the times you want.

Chapter 7

IDEAS FOR MONETIZING

One of the most exciting moments in running a business is making the first dollar. My first check from Google Adsense came around Christmas time. It was a check for $103.10. It was just enough to pay for my hosting costs, but it gave me such a tremendous sense of accomplishment.

The vast majority of blogs do not earn a significant income. To become a successful blogger takes hard work, time, and dedication. Most people are unwilling to devote much time and effort to their blogs.

A 2012 survey of 1,000 bloggers by Blogging.org found that only 9% of bloggers made a full-time income. Upwards of 81% never even made $100 from blogging. What this means is that you should not quit your day job to pursue blogging. A better tactic would be to start your blog on your free time, blog about your passion, and keep working at it. It takes time and dedication to build a significant following. You can only earn income if you have readers.

Diversification is essential. If you are serious about blogging for profit, don't let ad networks be your only source of revenue. This chapter has dozens of ideas for making money from your blog. Take advantage of as many sources of income as you can find. That is the only way you can build a solid blogging business.

The first part of this chapter has several ideas for finding advertising for your blog. Advertising is the most common way bloggers earn money. It is also easy to set up an advertising network on your blog.

The second part of the chapter introduces affiliate marketing. Affiliate marketing is a way you can earn commission from online sales. If you promote a product on your blog, you can get a part of the sales through affiliate marketing.

You can also sell products or services through your blog. The third section of the chapter provides ideas for different things you can sell on your blog. They range from physical products to digital products to services you can provide.

Advertising

Blogs are replacing print media like newspapers and magazines. Traditional print media made money by advertising within their pages. The easiest way to monetize a blog follows the same model. Companies pay you some money to put up advertisements on your blog.

A few factors go into how much you can make from advertisements. The most important factor is traffic. How many eyeballs see your blog each month? Measuring traffic can be tricky because not all traffic is equal. A blogger can use some slimy marketing tactics to drive traffic to a site, but the traffic will be low quality. On the other hand, a respected influencer may have a small group of loyal followers that buy everything she recommends on her blog. A skillful advertiser would take a few loyal followers over thousands of uninterested ones any day.

There are other important factors for advertising. The type of advertisements allowed matters. Some sites allow only text advertisements, while others may allow animations, sounds, and popups. Advertisement duration is also important. While some sites show an advertisement for only a moment, others keep it on the screen. Placement and size also play an important role. A full-page ad will cost much more than a line of text at the corner of a page.

Idea #99: Ad networks

There are several services that make it easy to add advertisements to your blog. Some of the more popular ones include Google AdSense (adsense.-google.com), Media.net (www.media.net), Chitika (www.chitika.com), Clicksor (www.clicksor.com), and Sovrn (www.sovrn.com).

Idea #100: Optimize your ads

When placing advertisements on your site, put the ads where people's eyeballs go. You might have to do some testing for different ad locations throughout your blog. In his book, *How to Make Money Blogging*, Bob Lotich attests that the most profitable spot to put AdSense ads is directly below the article title of a blog post. In How to Blog for Profit Without Selling Your Soul, Ruth Soukup confirms this, and adds that the next best advertisement positions are above, to the left, and at the bottom of your content. You should use this information as a starting point and run your own tests. The optimal settings may vary between different blogs. The only way to know for sure is to test it.

Note that if you have fewer than 50,000 page views per month, it's probably not worth your time to tweak your advertisements. Instead, concentrate on increasing your traffic before spending time tweaking advertisements.

Idea #101: Direct ad sales

Once your blog gains a presence in your niche, companies may begin reaching out to you to advertise. In this case, you can sell ad space directly to the company. The company would want to know exactly how much traffic you get so you can agree on a fair price.

While you can passively wait for companies to proposition you, you can also aggressively pursue direct advertisements. If this is the path you want to pursue, you need first to put together an advertising kit. It is a brochure that includes a description of your blog, traffic statistics, and specific advertising opportunities you offer. You may also want to go further and include testimonials, your bio, and your photo. You can find companies to work with by attending conferences and networking directly with company representatives.

Idea #102: Sponsorships

Sometimes, a company is willing to pay you to promote their brand. They can do this by sponsoring your blog for a certain amount of time or sponsoring individual blog posts. A company might also give you an exclusive coupon code that you can give your audience. If you have a podcast or newsletter, companies can also pay for you to promote their brands through those mediums.

Other times, a company might send you free products. They do this in hopes that you will show off the products to your audience or provide a positive review on your blog. They might even send you products to give away to your readers for free.

If you get a company sponsorship, it is important to disclose the relationship to your audience. In the United States, not providing disclosure is against the law. Be careful who you accept money from, because it will have an impact on your reputation. If your readers enjoy the products you recommend, you will gain loyalty; however, associating yourself with one bad brand can tarnish your reputation for a long time.

Idea #103: Real-world advertising

GoDaddy.com spent $2.4 million to air their first SuperBowl commercials in 2005. They gained more than 500,000 extra visitors to their website immediately following the advertisements. While you may not have the money for television commercials, it does show how effective offline ads can be.

Look into traditional advertising methods like print, radio, and television. If your message is compelling enough, people will remember your web address and look you up online. Something as simple as tacking your web address onto a bulletin board at your local grocery store may be a cost-effective way to drive new traffic to your site. Just make sure you are targeting the right audience. For example, a grocery store audience may be more interested in food- and home-oriented content.

Idea #104: Try a publicity stunt

Do something newsworthy or offbeat to get people's attention. There is a subtle art to publicity stunts, so you have to be careful. Stay too conservative, and nobody will notice. Go too controversial, and it may blow up in your face. But if you get it just right, your blog can go viral.

Public relations blogger Frank Strong recounts sending books with handwritten notes to people who gave his brand shout-outs on social media. While doing this never made his blog go viral, he did see a steady increase in his loyal fan base.

ConAgra Foods once staged a publicity stunt that backfired. In 2011, they invited bloggers to a free dinner at a fine restaurant. They didn't tell the guests that the food was not prepared by the chef, but was from ConAgra's line of frozen foods. They secretly recorded the guests' reactions to the food. The response from the bloggers was not what they expected. Many of the bloggers wrote negative reactions on their blogs because of ConAgra's perceived dishonesty.

Affiliate marketing

In affiliate marketing, you promote products and receive money for each sale you make. You are a salesperson making a commission.

There are many ways you can promote affiliate products. You can write a how-to post and link to the supplies needed. You can make YouTube videos to promote products. Or write comparisons between products. You can also write a shopping guide that shows people what to look for when buying a type of product like televisions or cameras.

Keep in mind that the same disclosure rules apply to affiliate marketing. When you include affiliate links in a blog post, you need to tell your readers that you will make some money if they buy through the links.

Idea #105: Become an Amazon affiliate

One of the biggest affiliate marketing programs is the Amazon Associates program (associates.amazon.com). You can earn a percentage of almost anything Amazon.com sells by including affiliate links on your blog. That means if your blog discusses a new video game, you can include an affiliate link to the game on Amazon. If a reader clicks your link to the game on Amazon and buys it, you will get a small percentage (usually around 4-6%) of the sale price.

Idea #106: Find affiliates outside of Amazon

Amazon is so big that they don't need your help for selling things. That's why they offer such low commission rates. If you want to earn more on commissions, you should seek out individual products to promote. Commission Junction (www.cj.com) is one of the largest affiliate networks out there. If you can find the right products to promote, you can make upwards of 50% commission. The downside is that you need to devote more time and effort to selling the product.

Another thing you can do is go to the websites of your favorite products and see if they have an affiliate program. If they do, they usually put the link at the bottom of the page. If they don't have an affiliate program, sometimes you can contact the company directly and ask if you can help sell their product for a percentage commission.

Selling products or services

You can sell products from your blog. They can be digital, physical, or service products.

The main benefit of digital products is that they can be delivered instantly. They don't take up space in your home. You can even automate the whole process so buyers can purchase the product and receive it without you having to do anything.

Many people still prefer physical products over digital. Having a physical product feels more real and valuable to them. They are products that people can put on their desks, touch, and give to others. Not everyone is comfortable with the digital versions of things. Most people will prefer to read physical books over e-books. Some things like food and equipment just can't be digitized. You can still sell these items from your blog.

You can also sell services from your blog. Services are not digital or physical. They are provided on the medium of time. They are conferences, live classes, special events, or consulting sessions.

You can accept payment from your blog using a payment service like PayPal (www.paypal.com) or Gumroad (www.gumroad.com).

Idea #107: Sell digital products

With the rising popularity of YouTube videos and podcasts, there is an increasing demand for music and voiceovers. People with video or audio shows need music and voiceovers for intros and outros. Audio Jungle (www.audiojungle.net) and iStock-

Photo (www.istockphoto.com) both sell audio clips. If you're an audio whiz, you can sell your audio files from those sites or your blog.

If you're a photographer, you can make money selling your photographs. Sites like iStockPhoto and Foap (www.foap.com) will sell your pictures for you. Or you can sell them directly from your blog.

If you can write your own themes and plugins, you can sell them on a site like Creative Market (www.creativemarket.com). You can also offer your code for free, but accept donations.

You can also sell domain names on Sedo (www.sedo.com). Sell blogs and websites on Flippa (www.flippa.com).

Idea #108: Sell information

Another type of digital product you can sell is an information product. Instead of selling finished media like photos, videos, or plugins, you sell information. The information can take many different forms. You could create an online course. You can run a live webinar or online workshop. You can also format the content as an e-book and sell it on your blog or Amazon's Kindle platform.

If you have been blogging for a while, you can curate your articles and edit them into e-book format. Add some additional writing to tie everything together. Upload it to Amazon Kindle Direct Publishing. Or convert it into a PDF file to sell on e-junkie (www.e-junkie.com) or your blog.

Idea #109: Repurpose your blog posts to sell

If you've been blogging for a while, you already have a lot of content. You can repurpose and repackage that content to sell. Even if the content is already free on your blog, some people will prefer to consume it in another format. Compile your best blog content into an e-book. Start a podcast based on your blog content. Put your most popular how-to posts together into an online course. Then you can sell the repurposed content on your blog.

Idea #110: Create a membership site

If you want to offer exclusive content from your blog, you can create a paid membership section using a WordPress plugin. The most popular WordPress membership plugin is Wishlist (www.wishlistproducts.com). A less capable, but free alternative is S2Member (www.s2member.com).

. . .

Idea #111: Sell custom-printed items

Many websites will print custom images onto products. You can upload your logo or other graphics to create branded clothing, bags, mugs, calendars, or almost anything. Two of the larger sites that do this are CafePress (www.cafepress.com) and Zazzle (www.zazzle.com). You can sell these customized products from your blog and have them made on demand.

Idea #112: Create your own games

The Game Crafter (www.thegamecrafter.com) lets you design your own board games or card games, then have them printed on demand. You can design game boards, rules booklets, and pick out pieces (like dice or pawns) to be included. Then, whenever someone orders the game, they will print it, package it, and mail it for you.

If all you need is custom playing cards, a company called MPC (www.makeplayingcards.com) can print high-quality playing cards that you can sell.

. . .

Idea #113: Host a live webinar

If your blog teaches something, you can offer more in-depth information through live webinars. You will need software like Crowdcast (www.crowdcast.io) or WebEx (www.webex.com). These operate much like remote classrooms. Students can pay for and register for your webinar in advance. Then, when the scheduled time comes, you log in and teach the webinar.

Chapter 8

IDEAS FOR COMING UP WITH IDEAS

This book can't provide an exhaustive list of every idea you can have. The best ideas are the ones not thought of yet.

You can borrow any idea out of this book without any modification. But I do hope that the ideas you find here act as a springboard for you to come up with even better ideas. As technology continues to change with the times, blog ideas will also change. Most of the content in this book will someday become outdated. But this chapter is evergreen.

This final chapter will give you ideas for coming up with ideas. You don't have to be a genius or a Bohemian artist to come up with good ideas. There are techniques for coming up with ideas that anyone can learn.

The first set of techniques will help get your brain in good shape for coming up with ideas. Your brain is like a muscle. It can tire out in exhaustion after a hard day of work. It can also atrophy when you don't use it enough. Use the exercises in this section to keep your brain in top shape.

The second group of techniques will help you find inspiration. Inspiration doesn't come from luck. You need to go out and find it. Inspiration comes from exposing yourself to new things and new information. This section will give you some ideas for where you can seek out inspiration.

The last set of techniques will teach you different ways to brainstorm ideas. Even with a healthy brain and inspiration, you won't get new ideas if you don't give yourself time to think. Brainstorming techniques are ways you can set aside time for coming up with ideas.

Supercharging your brain

If your brain is fatigued, it won't do you well for coming up with ideas. If you don't exercise it, it will be weak.

To be creative, you need to keep yourself healthy. It's

hard to think when you're in pain. It's also hard to think when you're sick, sluggish, and worried about things. It's only when you are free from worries, pain, and distractions that you can unleash the full power of your creativity.

Even being healthy is not enough if you don't actually use your brain. Like any other skill, creativity requires practice to master. If you practice creativity regularly, you will be able to harness it when you need it. Here are some things you can do to keep your brain in top shape.

Idea #114: Capture your ideas

Carry a pen and paper or smartphone with you everywhere you go. You need to have something to jot notes down with you at all times because you never know when you'll have a great idea. It can be as simple as a piece of paper and pencil in your pocket. Or it can be as sophisticated as a special app on your smartphone.

I like to carry my smartphone with me everywhere I go. I use Google Keep (www.google.com/keep) to take notes when ideas strike. Another popular choice is Evernote (www.evernote.com). While these two choices are special apps you can install, the notes app that comes standard with all smartphones will work as well.

Once you have a habit of taking notes on all your ideas, you also need to build a habit of reviewing your notes. What I do is go through my notes once a day. I would consider each note and decide what to do with it. I might paste it into a reference file, or a future projects list, or act on it immediately. Or if I decide that the note no longer has value, I would delete it. Once I've processed all my notes, I delete the note so I can start fresh the next day. Schedule a time each day to review your notes and take action on them.

Idea #115: Exercise

Exercise gets the blood flowing to your brain, which in turn helps boost creativity. For you to think to your full potential, you need to have a healthy body. A diseased body distracts the mind. Self-preservation takes priority over creativity. The less healthy you are, the more resources your brain diverts away from creative pursuits to sustain your life. It is hard to think when you are in pain. Your brain becomes sluggish when you are overweight.

To have a creative mind, you need to make daily

exercise a priority. Schedule exercise as early as possible in your day. Then you have the rest of the day to pursue your creativity.

Idea #116: Sleep

Sleep is just as important to your creativity as exercise. As you sleep, your brain collects its thoughts and clears away the toxins that built up during your waking hours. Your subconscious pieces together all the random bits of information, and tries to make sense of it.

Sometimes sleeping can help you get new ideas. You can use this to your advantage. Often, your brain works hardest on whatever you were thinking about before bed. Try thinking about your blog before falling asleep. You may wake up with some new ideas.

Idea #117: Change your environment

It's hard to come up with new ideas when you're looking at the same things all the time. Take a walk outside. Go somewhere you've never been before. Go to another room and sit on the floor for a while. Chances are, you will notice some things you've never noticed before. Noticing new things can help you think of new ideas.

Idea #118: Meditate

In a lot of ways, meditation is similar to sleep. You are taking control away from your conscious mind and letting go. If you have dozens of thoughts going through your head, it is hard to come up with new ideas. Meditation helps clear your thoughts to make room for new ones.

Meditation is easy and can be done in just a few minutes. Find a quiet spot and sit. Close your eyes. Breathe slowly and deeply while clearing your mind of thoughts. Concentrate on your breath. Whenever a thought enters your mind, imagine yourself grabbing that thought and blowing it away. Once your mind is clear and you are calm, you will be ready to work again with a fresh mind.

Finding inspiration

Ever notice how you get the best ideas in the shower or while you're reading? When your brain is at rest, it puts things together. It makes sense of things and creates new ideas. To make sure this works best, you need to put good content in your brain for it to work on in the subconscious.

There is a saying in computer science that goes, "garbage in, garbage out." If you put garbage information into a computer, you can only get garbage information out of it. The same applies to your brain, the most powerful computer of all. If you put bad information into your brain, you will always come to the wrong conclusions. And the opposite is also true. If you fill your brain with good information, you will come up with great ideas.

Idea #119: Do internet research

Next time you're surfing the web, instead of typing "funny cats" in the search box, try searching keywords related to your blog content. Hundreds of thousands of gigabytes of new content are uploaded to the internet each day. Search some keywords from your area of interest and let yourself get inspired by the content others have already created.

Steal ideas from other blogs you read. I don't mean that in a malicious way. Copying content is a punishable offense, but copying ideas is okay. People get ideas all the time, but few implement them. If you see something that seems to be working on someone else's blog, try it on your own blog.

Idea #120: Ask Amazon

Amazon (www.amazon.com) has a useful suggestion feature when you type in their search box. Type your topic into the Amazon search bar, and you will see the most popular searches beginning with the words you typed. If you run the search, you will then see what books have been written about the topic. This is all good information for knowing what kinds of information people are looking for.

Idea #121: Look at the trends

Some ideas pop into your head when you get new information. Sometimes, you will get new ideas by following the news and trends. It's easy to do these days with the internet.

Keep up with the news on news sites like Google News (news.google.com), BBC News (www.bbc.com), CNN (www.cnn.com), or popurls (www.popurls.com). Your niche likely has its own news sites. If you're having a tough time coming up with blog post ideas, try writing your thoughts about the latest article you read.

You can also keep up with the trends in your niche. Google Trends (www.google.com/trends) or TrendsMap (www.trendsmap.com) show things that are trending. Many social or news sites like Twitter (www.twitter.com) or YouTube (www.youtube.com) also have sections displaying topics that are currently trending.

Idea #122: Read

Prolific writers tend to read a lot. Stephen King reads seventy or eighty books a year, and he claims he's a slow reader. Reading is how people like Stephen King come up with so many ideas for their books. You should be spending at least as much time reading as you are writing. Reading is the input, and writing is the output. If you read too little, it will result in poor quality writing output.

Idea #123: Learn more about related topics

Knowledge is like a tree. It branches out into different disciplines. The disciplines branch out further into topics. Topics stem into niches. The niches spread further into leaves of information. And the tree is always growing and changing.

Once you've exhausted ideas from your topic, look at the branches off to the sides. Find the related issues. How can your blog's readers learn from similar but different fields? If your blog is about automotive repair, what can your readers learn from a car salesperson? It might surprise you how adjacent fields view your niche.

Idea #124: Go on a field trip

Sometimes to find inspiration, you must step outside and explore something new. Take a field trip. You don't have to go to a museum or somewhere new, though you can if you like. Even a trip to the local library or a walk around the mall can spark new ideas. Browse the magazines at the bookstore or library. Take a walk in the local park. Spend the afternoon at an art gallery. Inspiration often hits when you stop thinking so hard and take in new sights.

Brainstorming techniques

Brainstorming is the actual act of coming up with ideas. It is not keeping your brain sharp or a stroke of inspiration. You make a decision to come up with ideas at a particular time, then you sit down and try your hardest to come up with them.

There are many ways you can go through a brainstorming session. It can be a wild freethinking session of writing whatever comes to your head. Or it can be a structured collaborative effort between members of a team. There are benefits to both extremes.

The first rule of brainstorming is there are no bad ideas. Every idea that comes to mind should be considered, no matter how silly it seems at the outset. The point of brainstorming is not to find polished ideas, but to think out loud and work out solutions that may actually be good. Many million-dollar products have started out as ridiculous ideas taken too far.

Idea #125: Follow the Daily Practice

Writer and entrepreneur James Altucher always encourages people to follow the Daily Practice. The Daily Practice is coming up with ten ideas a day to keep your "idea muscle" strong. If you think of 10 ideas a day, that's 3,650 ideas a year. Following this simple practice, you will have thousands of new ideas in a matter of months. And you'll also have a strong idea muscle.

Idea #126: Group brainstorming

When you have a team working on a project, it is important to get feedback from each member. The simplest way to do a group brainstorming session is to have a meeting in person. One person will be the note taker, who will record every idea. Everyone then throws out any idea that comes to mind. Nobody is allowed to criticize any idea.

If the members of the group are more comfortable expressing ideas in writing, you can try this. Have everyone spend a few minutes writing down ideas. When the time is up, everyone trades sheets of paper and expands on those thoughts.

After the brainstorming session is complete, everyone can discuss which ideas are best. You can do further brainstorming sessions to develop the best ideas more.

Idea #127: Draw a mind map

A mind map is a diagram that organizes thoughts. You start out with a central concept and write that in the middle. Then you expand upon the central concept, drawing lines out of it for each new thought. For every thought you have, write down a description, keywords, or the name of the concept.

For thinking of new blog or article ideas, begin with your general topic in the middle. Then whatever ideas come to your head, write it down and draw a line out from where it came. In the end, the mind map should look like an octopus with idea-tentacles branching outward.

You can create mind maps with paper or a whiteboard. If you prefer, there are also many software solutions out there. Some popular ones you can use for free are Coggle (www.coggle.it), XMind (www.xmind.net), and FreeMind (freemind.sourceforge.net).

Idea #128: Explore another medium

There are advantages and disadvantages to each type of media. A blog post is well suited for delivering scannable text content to web browsers. Other types of media include e-books, audio books, online courses, slide presentations, and videos. Think about what other types of media you would like to try. How can you adapt content from your blog to other media? Or you can think of the reverse. How can you adapt other types of media content into blog posts?

Idea #129: Explore new technology

Imagine how different your online presence might be today if you were one of the first users of Facebook? What if you were the first to curate your blog posts into an e-book on Amazon Kindle? How would things be different if you started sending videos from your iPhone to your blog years ago?

Always be on the lookout for new platforms, new types of media, and new technology. Try new things. Think about how you can integrate new things into your blogging experience.

Idea #130: Make a lotus blossom

The Lotus Blossom technique was developed by Yasuo Matsumura. You start out with a central idea written in a square. There are eight boxes surrounding the central idea square. In each of the eight surrounding boxes, you write a related idea.

Draw a bigger box next to each of the eight surrounding boxes. In each of the bigger boxes, flesh out the related ideas.

This technique works well for coming up with a series of blog posts. The first article in the series will introduce the central concept. Then you can write the next articles in the series about the related topics.

Idea #131: PSFBB

PSFB is a brainstorming technique developed by an Australian company called Brain Mates (www. brainmates.com.au). It was further adapted by the Web Marketing Ninja in *The Blogger's Guide to Online Marketing* to include another B, for Barrier. PSFBB stands for Problem, Solution, Feature, Barrier, Benefits. You can use this technique to find ideas for what articles your readers need.

Start by listing problems your readers might have. For each problem, list a few possible solutions. For each solution, write a few features that will help you reach the solution. Features are the prerequisites for reaching the solution. They might include expert advice, people to talk to, instructions, services, or websites to visit. For each feature, write down barriers preventing people from getting the feature, or questions people may have about the feature. Finally, for each barrier, list the benefits of over- coming the barrier.

Now you should have a list of problems that branch out into many barriers. From here, you can write blog articles about how to overcome each of the barriers to solving each problem your readers have.

Chapter 9

CONCLUSION

I can't say that I've ever created a popular or profitable blog. But that was never my intention. I have always blogged for my own enjoyment and to help people with my content any way I could. There are no definitive metrics to measure whether a website is successful or not. You measure success by your goals and whether you've reached them.

This book provides a toolkit for you to differentiate your blog from the millions of others out there. It is not advice, but rather a listing of ideas and resources. If you look at my blog at ShockNotes.com (www.shocknotes.com), you will find that it doesn't follow most of the suggestions in this book. I choose only the ideas that I find most interesting. You should do the same.

I could delve into keyword analytics to determine the types of articles I write. I could schedule social media tweets and status updates to go out 18 times a day. I could use A/B testing to test ad placements. My blog might go viral and turn a massive profit if I did these things. Who knows? But I do none of these things because they don't align with my goals and don't interest me. It's different for everyone. Others might find doing those things fun.

But I might try some of these ideas in the future. Things are always changing. It's essential to the survival of your blog that you keep an experimental mindset. As long as you're always trying new ideas and nudging the boundaries ever further, your blog will always grow.

And that is the most powerful blog idea of all.

HAVE YOU JOINED THE MAILING LIST YET?

Want to see secret blog posts, get free and discounted books, and receive updated content about blogging and other topics? Join the Storm-Shock e-mail list.

It's free. I'll keep your email secret. Unsubscribe at any time.

And you'll also get access to some downloadable goodies.

Subscribe at www.smshock.com/list

MORE ON BLOGGING

A lot of research went into the making of this book. I've compiled a selection of the best resources I found. They are in no particular order, though I've put my favorites at the top of each list.

Books

Pro-Blogging Secrets: Strategies, Tips, and Answers You Need to Grow Your Blog and Earn More Money, by Bob Lotich

How to Blog for Profit without Selling Your Soul, by Ruth Soukup

My Blog Traffic Sucks! 8 Simple Steps to Get 100,000 Blog Visitors without Working 8 Days a Week, by Steve Scott

Problogger's Guide to Blogging for Your Business, by Mark Hayward

ProBlogger's Guide to your First Week of Blogging, by ProBlogger

Blogging All-in-One for Dummies, by Susan Gunelius

How to Start a Home-based Blogging Business, by Brett Snyder

How to Write Great Blog Posts that Engage Readers, by Steve Scott

How to Make Money Blogging: How I Replaced My Day Job with My Blog, by Bob Lotich

How to Work for Yourself: 100 Ways to Make the Time, Energy and Priorities to Start a Business, Book or Blog, by Bryan Cohen

The Blogger's Guide to Online Marketing: 31 Steps to a Profitable Blog, by The Web Marketing Ninja and Problogger

ProBlogger: Secrets for Blogging Your Way to a Six-Figure Income, by Chris Garrett

How to Start a Successful Blog in One Hour, by Steve Scott

Blog Wise: How to Do More with Less, by Darren Rowse

How to Find a Profitable Blog Topic Idea, by Steve Scott

WordPress To Go, by Sarah McHarry

How To Start A Profitable Authority Blog In Under One Hour, by Passive Marketing

How to Make $1,000 Per Day Blogging Part Time, by Chris Karlas

Blogging, by Efron Hirsch

Blogging: Blogging Blackbook, by Jason Wolf

Websites

Problogger (www.problogger.net)

Copyblogger (www.copyblogger.com)

Blogging Your Passion (www.bloggingyourpassion.com)

SEOBook (www.seobook.com)

Successful Blog (www.successful-blog.com)

Chris Garrett on New Media (www.chrisg.com)

Chris Brogan (www.chrisbrogan.com)

Duct Tape Marketing (www.ducttapemarketing.com)

Moz Blog (www.moz.com/blog)

Small Biz Survival (www.smallbizsurvival.com)

The Smart Passive Income Blog (www.smartpassiveincome.com)

ViperChill (www.viperchill.com)

Blogging Tips (www.bloggingtips.com)

Daily Blog Tips (www.dailyblogtips.com)

Basic Blog Tips (www.basicblogtips.com)

The Blog Herald (www.blogherald.com)

My Blogger Lab (www.mybloggerlab.com)

My Blogger Tricks (www.mybloggertricks.com)

Podcasts

Problogger Podcast, hosted by Darren Rowse (www.problogger.com/podcast)

Smart Passive Income, hosted by Pat Flynn (www.smartpassiveincome.com/podcasts)

Blogging Your Passion, hosted by Jonathan Milligan (www.bloggingyourpassion.com)

How They Blog, hosted by Kat Lee (www. howtheyblog.com)

Online Marketing Made Easy, hosted by Amy Porterfield (www.amyporterfield.com/category/podcast)

Online Articles

Blogs Falling in an Empty Forest, by Douglas Quenqua (www.nytimes.com/2009/06/07/fashion/07blogs.html)

Blogging Statistics, Facts and Figures in 2012 – Infographic, by Jeff Bullas (www.jeffbullas.com/2012/08/02/blogging-statistics-facts-and-figures-in-2012-infographic)

Can You REALLY Make Money Blogging? [7 Things I Know About Making Money from Blogging], by Darren Rowse (www.problogger.net/can-you-really-make-money-blogging-7-things-i-know-about-making-money-from-blogging)

Use No Bad Ideas Brainstorming to Come Up With Ideas, by Jason Zook (www. jasondoesstuff.com/brainstorming)

GoDaddy traffic soars, by Krysten Crawford (money. cnn.com/2005/02/08/technology/godaddy)

10 Timeless Creative PR Ideas, by Frank Strong

(www.swordandthescript.com/2013/12/timeless-creative-pr-ideas)

The PR Stunt that Failed and Lessons for Good Blogger Relations, by Mana Ionescu (www.lightspandigital.com/blog/the-pr-stunt-that-failed-and-lessons-for-good-blogger-relations)

23 Must See Free Blogging Platforms, by Jerry Low (www.webhostingsecretrevealed.net/blog/blogging-tips/23-must-see-free-blogging-platforms)

The 18 best blogging sites and publishing platforms on the internet today, by Owen Williams (www.thenextweb.com/businessapps/2015/05/11/the-18-best-blogging-and-publishing-platforms-on-the-internet-today)

The 11 Best Free Blog Sites, by Kristen Bousquet (www.stylecaster.com/best-free-blog-sites)

The 12 best free blogging platforms, by Craig Grannell (www.creativebloq.com/web-design/best-blogging-platforms-121413634)

Different types of blog, by Mike Ham (www.slideshare.net/pi0540735/different-types-of-blog-11609124)

The Complete Guide to Building Your Blog Audience, by Neil Patel and Aaron Agius (www.

quicksprout.com/the-complete-guide-to-building-your-blog-audience)

38 Websites and Blogs That Pay Writers $100 Per Article and More (Updated for 2015), by Jennifer Mattern (www.allindiewriters.com/blogs-pay-writers-100-per-article)

20 Sites To Get Paid For Writing And Blogging – Best Of, by Brian Voo (www.hongkiat.com/blog/sites-to-get-paid-blogging)

How To Monetize Your Blog By Repurposing Content, by Natalie Sisson (www.problogger.net/monetize-blog-repurposing-content)

10 Sure-Fire Headline Formulas That Work, by Brian Clark (www.copyblogger.com/10-sure-fire-headline-formulas-that-work)

The Lotus Blossom Creative Technique, by Robert Riley (www.thoughtegg.com/lotus-blossom-creative-technique)

ABOUT THE AUTHOR

 Steve Alvest grew up with an intense interest in two seemingly unrelated subjects—science and art. He graduated from Virginia Tech with an MBA in information technology, a B.S. in computer science, and minor degrees in history, mathematics, and studio art. He spent a decade working at the United States Patent & Trademark Office, judging the originality of other people's ideas and inventions. Steve now writes in the suburbs of Washington, D.C. with his wife, dog, and three kids.

Connect with Steve Alvest online:

Website: www.SteveAlvest.com

Email: steve@stormshock.com

ALSO BY STEVE ALVEST

The Life Actionbook: Tools and Actions for Personal Development (smshock.com/lifeactionbook)

Summary of Think and Grow Rich: The Wisdom of Napoleon Hill (smshock.com/summarythink)

Summary of How to Win Friends and Influence People: Lessons from Dale Carnegie (smshock.com/summaryfriends)

www.ingramcontent.com/pod-product-compliance
Lightning Source LLC
Chambersburg PA
CBHW051242050326
40689CB00007B/1032